PERMISSION TO BE ME

RISING FROM THE SHAME OF MY CHILDHOOD

TRACE KINGHAM

Editorial Project Management: Karen Rowe, www.karenrowe.com

Cover Design: Angela Hammersmith, hammersmithgraphics.com
Interior Layout: Ljiljana Pavkov, bookwormsdesign.com

Printed in the United States

ISBN: 978-0-9970194-1-4 (paperback)
ISBN: 978-0-9970194-2-1 (digital)

To my boys—
I hope you will follow your truth!

Contents

PERMISSION
TO BE ME

Author's Note

I discuss and approach my identity in this memoir from my experience and perspective as a gay male coming of age in the 1970s and 1980s. The terminology used in this book and around gender has changed since I was growing up, but the message is relevant for all transgender, gender-nonconforming, and gender-questioning youth, who still encounter pervasive discrimination today. I've used the gender-neutral pronouns "they/them" when gender preference was unknown or not directly stated.

To protect the privacy of others, some names have been changed. This book is a reflection of my own personal truth and how I experienced the world at a particular point in my life. I have no doubt the people who went through these same moments walked away with entirely different understandings and their own truths regarding what happened.

Prologue

I wrote this book for my fifteen-year-old self. For the child in Anywhere, America, or beyond who feels isolated or stifled by their surroundings—like there is no one in their family or community who understands who they are. For the teenager who doesn't feel celebrated for their identity, who feels overlooked or mislabeled, i.e., like "the weird one."

I also wrote this book for adults who are struggling to celebrate and appreciate themselves; maybe all those messages you've received throughout life from the outside world are so deeply ingrained that you have come to believe them about yourself.

You might not feel it is safe to fully be yourself. You might find yourself in dangerous situations while trying to find a place where you fit in. You might not even know who you really are yet, nor have discovered that you're not alone.

You want to belong.

You want permission from those around you to be yourself.

You want to be seen.

I wanted all those things, too. My hope is that this book will help you realize that being different is your superpower. You are not alone. And if you're suffering, things can and *will* get better.

While you may not feel you have permission to be seen, from loved ones or the community in which you live, I hope that this book helps you give yourself permission to be you, in ways that are safe and healthy.

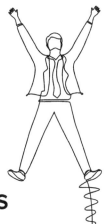

CHAPTER 1:

Not Like the Others

I've known I was different since Christmas Eve, 1973.

Blizzard-like conditions engulfed Hilliard, Ohio, but nothing was going to stop us from reaching Granny's house, thirty miles down the road and one county over. We slipped and slid our way down the road, my older brother—Rick—and me in the backseat of Mom's Rambler, not wearing seatbelts, with the presents for our grandparents, aunts, uncles, cousins, and each other between us. My dad wasn't with us; my mom had left him in 1971, but even before then, she always drove, no matter what.

Finally, we arrived. We gathered the presents and Mom's amazing pies and desserts in our arms and made our way out of the cold and blinding snow and through the garage door of our beloved Granny's house. Granny, Grandpa, and my aunt, uncle, and younger cousins were already there. Mom took off her long, wool coat, and my brother and I had to take them along with our coats to the guest bedroom and properly place them before we could make our way to the family. Right away, we saw that the large dinner table had already been set with her best dishes—handmade by Granny herself in her basement ceramics studio—and decorated with ceramic Christmas trees. Antique glass bowls were filled with nuts and mints. The savory scent of turkey and ham filled the air, punctuated with the sweet smell of chocolate chip cookies. Normally, we had to ask for cookies and candy when we visited, but at Christmas, sweets were ours for the taking. In the corner was a smaller, square table set for just us kids, with each place setting designed specially for each child. My eyes quickly scanned the table. *Are all the decorations there?* Yep, without exception, Granny had it ready for all of us!

"Merry Christmas!" Granny, my mother's mom, interrupted my thought and gave us each a hug. "You can set all the presents by the Christmas tree." We always had a live tree at home, askew with lots of gaps and holes and our house cat to survive, but Granny's artificial tree had such a great shape, with perfect lighting and ornaments that always coordinated. The tree skirt was white, and everything was neat as a pin—just like my Granny!

Rick and I ran over to the tree and placed all our presents underneath, then looked at all the labels among the heap of gifts already there. When we found the ones with our names, we tried to guess their contents by sizing up their dimensions and how heavy they were. It was magical. I was a small-statured seven-year-old; the tree, all lit up, stretched to the ceiling and felt twenty feet tall. A tall grandfather clock stood next to the Christmas tree and chimed every fifteen minutes, ticking off the time until we could open presents.

It felt like we had to wait forever.

"When are we gonna open presents?" I asked impatiently.

"After dinner, Tracy." Tracy was my given name at birth; in college, I changed it to my nickname, Trace. "Same as always." While the women finished cooking, Grandpa tried to distract us by encouraging us to play with his train set in the guest bedroom. When dinner was finally ready, we kids ate so fast and felt discouraged when the adults didn't do the same.

"We're done eating. Can we open presents now?" we'd take turns asking.

"Not yet. We'll be done eating soon." We couldn't believe how much talking the adults were doing, or how long it took them to finish their meals. At last, the adults brought the dining room chairs into the living room, seated in a circle with the kids gathering on the floor, squealing and giggling as Granny and Grandpa passed out the gifts: presents for the kids, envelopes with cash for the adults. They were like carrots dangling in front of our faces, because we couldn't open any of them until everyone got their presents. When the last gift was distributed, we set about tearing the wrapping to shreds. One by one, I heard the joy in everyone else's voice.

"Oh, wow, an Easy-Bake oven!" my cousin Lisa cried out. "Thanks, Granny and Grandpa!"

"Oh, thank you so much!" my mom exclaimed to her parents, a huge wad of cash in hand.

"A remote-control truck!" my brother exclaimed, running over to thank Granny and Grandpa. Everyone set about playing with their new toys. Except me. Beneath the wrapping paper of my gift was a John Deere toy truck. I fought tears in my eyes. All that anticipation...*for this*? The bubble had burst. *I don't want a toy truck*, I thought. I looked longingly over at my cousin's Easy-Bake oven. *Why can't I have that?* I wasn't into dolls or Barbies, but I coveted anything to do with sewing or baking. Nonetheless, I said thank you to my grandparents and got up to give them a hug, because that's what I'd seen my brother do. I didn't want to hurt their feelings; I loved them so much. *But why don't they understand what I want?* I thought to myself.

That's when I started to realize that something was different inside of me. I was a boy, so I was treated as a boy, but I didn't want boy things. I looked around the room at the smiling and expectant faces and thought, *They're not seeing who I am.* Something about me wasn't being celebrated. Somehow, I knew that if I wanted to receive their adoration and acceptance, I had to pretend to be someone I was not.

That was the beginning of the painful practice of pushing down what was inside of me—the real me.

The inner dialogue began: "Okay, so if they want to see me as a boy, then I have to do some boy things because I want my family's love and acceptance." I watched my siblings and cousins having a blast and began mimicking them. From then on, most of my childhood became about pretending.

***

I can give my parents—and any parent of that era—a little grace. They harbored no malice; we were products of the '70s. I was born into a time and place and narrative where boys got trucks and train sets, while girls got dolls and crafts. Boys wore blue; girls wore pink. Boys behaved one way, girls another. It was sugar and spice and everything nice. There were no gender-expansive pronouns like we have today, just he and she, boy and girl. And if you were different, if you didn't fit inside the box, you were looked down upon. There was no gray area for gender roles; you were either very feminine or very masculine. Gender was binary, period. If you broke away from those norms, you were taunted and teased. Even tomboys were looked at and treated differently. "You're a little funny" was a phrase I remember hearing often.

As a child, I didn't know the word "gay." I didn't know anybody who was gay. In the '50s, '60s, and into the '70s, gay men were so closeted that they were marrying women and having kids. They were doing anything they could to cover up their sexuality, to hide who they were. But sometimes people knew anyway. If someone in the community was a little different, there were whispers. *Well, he lives alone. He's a little off. He bats for the other team.* There was a shameful tone behind those comments. Just as *Sesame Street* sang, "One of these things is not like the others," if someone was different, they didn't belong.

I felt like an outcast in our community. We lived in Unionville Center, Ohio—a farming community about thirty miles northwest of Columbus, with only fifty to seventy-five households. There was nothing but a tiny post office and general store, not even a traffic light. It was a town where the opinions of the community and the people you went to church with and saw every day were what mattered. In rural Ohio, there was no safe space to be different. It was dangerous to be gay. There was an overarching farm-boy mentality; if you were different, you got beaten up. If you didn't conform to the norms of rural Ohio, you were snapped back into shape. In our rural community, it would have been a death sentence for an older gentleman to come out and say, "I'm gay," or to live an openly gay lifestyle. The closet was still very closed in the 1970s.

As a flamboyant kid, I was accepted to a certain degree, but not fully celebrated. So much was happening with the gay movement outside of rural Ohio that I was not privy to; I was too young to know. The Stonewall Uprising happened in New York City in 1969, followed by the first Gay Pride marches in New York, Los Angeles, and Chicago in 1970. Even the nearby city of Columbus, Ohio, passed a law protecting gay rights in 1974, but I didn't hear about that. Besides, moving to a big city wasn't an option as a kid. This was my life, and I had to figure out how to get through it and stay safe.

Starting with that Christmas Eve, I had to quickly learn how to assess a situation and play the role of someone I was not. It was stifling and saddening; I was always worrying about what people were going to think and what people were going to do to me. At that age, it played a big role—and continued to, well into my adult life. To this day, I have to help that inner child overcome being afraid of others and caring what they will think about me for being myself. I did not feel safe outside of the house growing up, and I found refuge with safe people and my family, but it was always a lot of work. It pains me to think that children today still have to navigate this type of environment; no child should have to live in fear of being themselves. Gender-nonconforming kids were born into this world to have a full experience, just like everyone else.

The hardest part for me was seeing my brother, sister, and cousins being celebrated for who they were, and getting to just be themselves. *Why can't I be me?* I wondered. The self-hatred kicked in. *Why me? Why am I different? Why was I chosen to be this way?* I couldn't help it; being different was not something that I'd learned. It was just who I was.

I'm sure there were other people around me who were struggling with who they were and how they felt they needed to be. I didn't think about it at the time, but my mother must have been one of them. She became pregnant with my brother at sixteen years old, out of wedlock. Rather than leave town, she married my father, whom she'd met in high school. He was a couple of years older than she was. How quickly she had to grow up, yet she had no worldly experience. When I came along, she was still just nineteen years old.

My mother came from a very sophisticated society position in rural Ohio. My grandparents were a highly influential couple in the community. They co-owned a bowling alley, my grandfather owned a tractor dealership, and Granny taught ceramics classes; they were the socialites of the community. They were big farmers and prominent members of the Lutheran church, and that put a lot of pressure on my mom and my aunt. At her core, my mom was a nonconformist. She wanted to get the hell out of that town and that household; she found her mother very controlling. But both she and her mother worried a lot about what other people thought, so that kept her in her place.

After my parents got married, they moved into a brick house next to my grandparents' house. In July of '66, while my mom was eight months pregnant with me, a tornado came through town. As my mother was running to the outside bunker—like the one in *The Wizard of Oz*—the stairs were wet from the heavy rain, and she fell. She was rushed to the hospital after the storm. They were worried about me, but both my mother and I were fine. The house, not so much. When my parents and brother came out of the bunker, all that was left of their home was a heap of bricks and debris. All their possessions were gone. To this day, my brother, who was only three when the tornado struck, has a fear of storms.

My great-grandparents' two-story white house was fine, as was the vacant home on their property, into which my family was invited to move. It hadn't been lived in for years; my brother remembers that it smelled like mildew and there were bugs everywhere. My parents didn't want to live there either but felt they had no choice at the time. So they cleaned it up and moved in. After I was born, they found a small split-level house in Hilliard, where a lot of our family members lived, and we moved there. The home was behind the big Lutheran church, with its imposing brown steeple. We didn't live there long, however, before moving to Worthington, which is another suburb of Columbus. That's the house where I remember sitting in front of the TV, listening to my parents bicker and fight.

My mother always told me that I was wanted; I think she was very happy with my dad at the time I was born. I know that my dad really loved my mom. He told me later in life that he did, and I think he still holds a special place in his heart for her today. As a housewife, I think she felt stifled because Dad wouldn't let her work until it became financially necessary. The stories I hear about my dad from my mom are that he was very controlling; it seemed like she had married back into what she had been trying to run away from with her mother. I know that couples have their trials and tribulations, and each person has a point of view on circumstances in the relationship. But I believe my dad and my mom were both coming into the relationship with as much good intent as they could with the information they had at the time. When I was four or five years old, she got a job at a ceramics studio, which happened to be where she met the man who would become my stepdad. They had an affair, and the next thing I knew, we moved from the house in Worthington to a two-bedroom apartment in Hilliard with a stranger named Tom.

The change happened in the middle of the night. I shared a room with my brother, Rick. We heard our parents fighting, and then Mom burst through our door, grabbed Rick and me, and told us to get in the car. There we were, sitting in the backseat of the Rambler, driving to Granny's house, just like at Christmas, only there was no air of joy or antic- ipation; instead, I remember confusion and fear. I remember my brother, fearful as well, comforting me. He was a good big brother, which I appreciate to this day. We stayed with Granny for what felt like a long time but probably wasn't—as children we had no real concept of time—before the move to Tom's. It was a very abrupt change for a kid. It was also hard on my brother, who was eight years old. He began lashing out, screaming at my mother, "I hate you!" The apartment was small and cramped. I remember talking to my dad on the kitchen phone, staring at the avocado-green appliances, wishing for some privacy. I missed my dad a lot, and the calls were a reminder of what I was missing. While I thought we would go back to living with my dad, days turned into weeks and weeks turned into months—I finally came to the realization that we weren't going to be living with him any longer.

Dad would pick us up in his Corvette for weekend visits. I'd have to sit on my brother's lap because the Corvette was a two-seater. My relationship with my dad was okay; I wouldn't say it was close, because I was so young when we moved out. Besides, I just wasn't into the same things. My dad's a car guy; he loved rebuilding engines. My brother did too, so it was easier for them to bond. It wasn't long, however, before Dad got a girlfriend who became his wife, and then he became a father of two more sons. It was difficult to integrate us into their new family unit, due to the custody arrangement of only being with them every other weekend. Still, they tried to make us feel welcome. My stepmom was really sweet and embraced my brother and me openly from the very beginning. When I met her, she had a warmth to her personality that I liked. But I did envy my two half brothers for being able to live with both their parents.

My mom's side of the family was growing, too. Mom and Tom had my sister, Sarah, in 1974. A bassinet was added to their bedroom, until it quickly became clear we needed a bigger house. So, Tom left the ceramics studio, started working at the Sears warehouse, and bought a home with my mom, just behind the apartment we'd been living in. I again shared a room with my brother; we slept in a bunk bed and did what we could to carve out our own spaces.

Rick, Sarah, my mom, and Tom were my primary family unit. Tom didn't make a whole lot of money at his job as a forklift operator at the Sears warehouse in Columbus, so Mom had to work. She had left the ceramics studio when we moved from Hilliard to Unionville Center because the commute had become too long. Not long after moving, she got a job as a school bus driver.

Money was a big issue in our house. One time, my mother approached my brother and me crying, asking for money from our piggy banks to pay the mortgage. It was a very difficult time. It scared me; I had never seen my mom so vulnerable. I could feel her shame and embarrassment and wanted to comfort her. I don't remember if I said it out loud or just thought it, but what I remember going through my head was: "It's okay, Mom. If that's what we have to do, that's what we have to do." I don't know if I'd ever seen my mother cry before then, so I knew it was serious. It surprised me that she was so desperate because I had never felt like we'd ever had to go without. Our freezer was always full of meat and popsicles and ice cream sandwiches. We always had birthday parties and birthday cake, which we'd make ourselves—not the kind that you purchase at a full-service grocery store today. Perhaps that month had been extra difficult because of home repairs; we lived in an old farmhouse, and I remember constantly hearing about things that needed fixing, followed by the cost of the repairs and laments about how expensive they were.

Although I was a product of love, I didn't feel like I always fit in. I never really felt that I had permission to be myself truly. I wasn't close to my dad, and I wasn't Tom's son. Tom was a fisherman and an army guy. We went camping, canoeing, and fishing; I didn't like any of it. I did it because I had to, but it wasn't me. On the other hand, my mom was right there next to Tom, hunting, fishing, canoeing, and camping. Dad, by contrast, has probably never held a gun in his life. As for me, I loved the clean and tidy life of a homemaker. I liked the things my grandmothers did. I wanted to be in the kitchen, wearing an apron, baking cakes and pies.

Looking back, Mom must have known what it felt like to not fit in, too. I don't want to diminish her love or any of her efforts. She tried her best, under difficult circumstances. She was a baby, raising babies. I feel she tried to be very fair with us, but I still wasn't sure where I belonged. I'm sure I was a bit effeminate as a young boy, but once I started presenting myself as more and more effeminate, it became hard for her to know what to do with me. She must have battled with unconscious questions, such as "How do I protect this child?" I felt her love, but I also felt her shame—or at least her not knowing what to do as the parent of a gay son in rural Ohio in the '70s. I probably felt what she felt from her mother when she got pregnant out of wedlock. *What will people think?*

Despite feeling like I didn't fit in, I always felt loved. Mom was physically affectionate and would hug all three of us all the time. She'd have a big smile on her face when we came home from school, and she made us treats and wrote us cards for Valentine's Day, Easter, and our birthdays. I remember always loving special smaller holidays because we had no expectations, and Mom would often surprise us. We would get home from school and see her amazing crafting and baking work on the table for the kids on these Hallmark holidays. Apart from the year when we cut down a Christmas tree from my great-grandmother's woods on her farm, every year we would all go together to buy a tree at the Christmas tree lot. No matter how poor we were, there were always gifts and treats for us.

Looking back, I was lucky. It could have been so much worse. In my adult life, I've heard horror stories of parents kicking their children out of the home for being themselves or not conforming to the social norms of the time. Thank goodness that wasn't my story. Mom told all us kids that she loved us, and she treated us the same in so many ways. There was just this *one* way in which I felt I was treated differently: my brother was celebrated for being a boy, my sister was celebrated for being a girl, but I didn't feel celebrated for being who I was.

CHAPTER 2:

Going Against the Norm

It's ironic that my parents named me Tracy—a common girl's name. I was teased for my name even before I showed signs of being effeminate. "That's a girl's name!" my cousins would say. "That's a name for sissies!" Mom said my name came from the 1960s sitcom *Please Don't Eat the Daisies*, featuring a family with twin boys named Tracey and Trevor. "Why didn't you name me Trevor?" I asked. She just laughed and said she preferred Tracy.

When my sister was first born, I was a little resentful. She got all my mom's attention. But as she got older, she played with dolls and played house, and I'd play along with her. Despite her being eight years younger than me, we were very close.

While my sister and I played house, my brother would be out in the garage, tinkering with something. He was always covered in dirt or grease. Tom would be out gallivanting, hunting and fishing, a true outdoorsman. By the time I was ten, I was not presenting as a typical hetero boy. I'd watch my mother sew or cook, and I'd ask, "Can I help?" An inner voice had a burning desire: *Can I be a part of this?* In those moments, I had sparks of knowing, *This is what I like.* I liked to sew, I liked crafts, and I loved to bake with my mom. To her credit, my mom nurtured those parts of me, once I started showing more interest. She never said, "No, you can't do that." She never shamed me for liking things; we had some really nice bonding experiences sharing those hobbies. She bought me all the things I needed to bake—baking pans, an apron, hot pads. I had access to art supplies. Mom showed me how to do a lot of things that would be deemed nontraditional for a boy. In those moments, the world disappeared, and it was just the two of us crafting. I have the same sort of memories with my stepmom, too.

With Mom, I'd sit at the sewing machine, and she'd show me how to thread the needle. I had just learned the basics when she gave me a little bit of money and took me to Joann Fabrics. It was Christmastime, and I wanted to make her a gift. I decided to make her a bathrobe, since she didn't have one. I got the pattern and terry cloth fabric and kept them hidden from my mom in the store, on the drive home, and as I sat at the sewing machine.

"Just be careful," she warned me as she left the room so that I could have the privacy I asked for.

I quickly learned that terry cloth is extremely difficult to work with for the skill level I had at the time. A bathrobe was very ambitious, but I set about the task. What I didn't realize but soon learned is that patterns are sized, and you have to cut them down to a specific measurement. I made the largest robe that the pattern allowed. After several days of working on it, I finished the robe and boxed it up using old newspapers and some ribbon to make it as beautiful as I could.

When my mother opened it up and saw the robe, I could see the confusion on her face. She tried it on and exclaimed, "Well, two of me could fit in here!" but she smiled. Everyone laughed. She could see how proud I was and how much I wanted to learn how to sew. She went on to teach me buttonholing and zippering. Here my mother was, teaching me how to do things that weren't going to be accepted out in the world. Looking back, I realize how lucky I was, but at the same time, there was an unspoken rule that I couldn't do these things outside of the home. I couldn't share what I'd made with other kids, or I would be made fun of.

Then there was baking. Granny was always in the kitchen baking something, and she passed that tradition down to my mother, who loved making homemade rolls, breads, cakes, pies, cookies, and desserts. My mom used to work in the kitchen at the bowling alley my grandparents owned; she started out making hamburgers but went on to make pies. Everybody loved her pies; one day, when she didn't make them, Granny was upset with her because the customers were so disappointed—a testament to how good of a baker my mom is!

Granny would enter her pies into baking contests at the fair in Madison County, where she lived. I have newspaper clippings featuring Granny as an award-winning baker. To this day, when I bake, I see her smiling in those clippings! Then a few weeks later, Mom would enter her yeast rolls or pies or her red velvet cake in the Union County Fair. When I was little, Mom showed me how to make the icing and mix the dough. I would stand on a little stool and dip the measuring cup into the flour; she taught me how to level off the top and get the measurement exact. She had an old, green, stand mixer that I liked to watch spin around and around until the batter came out creamy. Those moments with my mom were wonderful.

When I was around twelve years old, Mom taught me how to make a chocolate cake with chocolate icing made from sour cream. We tested it with the family, and everyone loved it. "Can I enter this in the county fair contest, Mom?" I asked. She helped me with the paperwork, but I baked the cake myself. It looked fantastic—I was so proud! We brought it to the fair. There was a white barn with white shelves lined up inside, with a section for cakes and a section for pies. I placed my cake next to the little placard that had my number on it—there were no names, so none of the judges could know whose was whose. I watched anxiously as the judges went around later that day and tested every cake, looking for texture, consistency, and taste. It felt like forever before they shared the results.

"And the winner of the blue ribbon is...cake number five!"

I couldn't believe it! I had won the blue ribbon—with my very first cake! The fair then auctioned off the cakes to local restaurants that would serve them. The restaurant that bought my cake paid me twenty dollars for it, which I thought was incredible. I earned twenty dollars for doing something I loved! I used the money to go shopping with my mom to buy more baking pans and supplies. Looking back, I did feel celebrated in that moment. I remember women coming up to me that day at the county fair to congratulate me. There were also women who didn't talk to me; they may have thought I cheated them out of the award. Since my name, Tracy, was more familiar as a female name, any newspaper publication announcing the winners didn't make it obvious that I was a boy, so I didn't have the community at large to contend with. I don't think the kids at my school even knew I had entered. I don't have any recollection of feeling ashamed or embarrassed that I was a boy who liked to bake, despite being the only boy ever in the kitchen. My brother didn't bake, my cousins didn't bake, and even my sister didn't bake. Grandma Kingham—my dad's mom—did, though.

Grandma Kingham was a bookkeeper for grocery stores in the local area. She and Grandpa

Kingham lived in a ranch-style home with an office set up in the basement, including a typewriter and a heavy-duty electric calculator that would spit out tape with numbers. What I remember most about Grandma Kingham is she always had an iced tea in hand, with a straw. And, she loved to bake. She made the most amazing strawberry pie! She taught me how to make a Texas sheet cake. When I got older, she even taught me how to drive a car—she drove an automatic, whereas my mom only bought stick shifts, so I used Grandma's car for my driving test. She also loved to shop; we had a tradition of looking through the ads in the Sunday paper after Thanksgiving and asking each other, "Would you like this? How about this?" She always gave me permission to be myself. I remember those moments of living without shame so vividly. My therapist told me that these moments of acceptance with my grandmothers had been enough to keep me from feeling worthless and depressed. Studies consistently tell us that children who feel accepted by family members have a heightened sense of family connectedness, higher self-esteem, and fewer psychosocial challenges, such as anxiety and depression (Ansari & Qureshi, 2013; Dwairy, 2010). I could "turn off" the pretending I had become so accustomed to at school, and I would come to life.

Baking was a thread that ran throughout the women in my family. My mother liked having me as her kitchen helper. I baked all throughout my teenage years. "You should be a pastry chef," she suggested. She could see me having a career as a professional baker, although I couldn't see it for myself. I still love baking to this day, but it has always been just a hobby for me. Despite her encouragement to pursue baking, I had a feeling that I was not making my mother as proud as I would have by conforming. I don't know if that feeling was coming from her, or from the world around me, since I never felt safe sharing my love of baking with my peers. Baking was something I did only at home, and among older women. It was a rare world I could get lost in where I felt like I belonged.

***

There was one other place besides the kitchen where I felt a sense of safety and belonging. Granny had a ceramics studio in the basement of her home. In the seventies, ceramics was a pretty popular activity. In the middle of the basement was a big brick wall that supported the house; on one side was the laundry area with kilns, a large sink, and all of her molds and "slip." We'd pour the slip into the molds, let it sit for a specific amount of time, and then dump it into a bucket. The molds were some of the most popular items. On the other side of the basement was a long table with chairs; on the table were shells of ceramic projects that ladies in the community could come and purchase. A couple nights a week, Granny would open her garage door, and women would come in and fill the basement with their chitchatting, cackling, and giggling. Granny would float around and help them glaze their selections; she was an expert in ceramics. She had all the products, brushes, and tools that were needed to create various effects.

She was meticulous with organization. I think I got my attention to detail from spending time in Granny's basement. The studio was spotless; everything had its place. Brushes were kept in jars according to size and shape; any brush, sponge, or tool that someone used had to be washed before being put away. Sheets of paper were spread out on the tables and discarded at the end of each day. To my delight, I was often able to help her in the studio. Because my mom worked a lot in those days, I was frequently at Granny's between the ages of eight and twelve. As I got older, Granny gave me more responsibilities. I would pick up brushes or glaze for the ladies, keep a running list of their purchases, run the cash register, wrap up their purchases, and go around doing whatever else was needed. It was so exciting to be in a room full of women! I felt like I could be more myself around women than when men were present. I wasn't worried about safety in those moments; I don't remember hearing anyone whispering about me. I was just a cute little boy helping his grandmother.

Granny trusted that I knew how to do things properly, so I believed in myself, too. I even demanded respect from my cousins in that space. I'd be down there playing "cash register" with my cousins when no one else was around, acting like the big kahuna, because it was my space. I was large and in charge, and I probably came across as a little bossy, saying, "No, the cash needs to face up and be in order. Don't touch that; it's fragile." The underlying message was: *This is my territory. I'm going to show you how it's done.* I was protective of the space, because it was one of the few places where I felt I belonged and had some control. It was where I could see myself in the world.

I'd help Granny outside of the studio, too. We'd go to Karschener's Ceramics in Columbus, where my mother had worked and where she'd met Tom. We'd get supplies that I'd help her load into her Lincoln Continental. Even though we were still in the community where I grew up, being with Granny felt like being in a little safe zone. She didn't look down on me for being different; I always felt loved by her. She was very proud of who I was, even years later, after I came out. She accepted my husband; she accepted my kids. Maybe her wisdom came with age, but her acceptance of me is remarkable when I think about who she was in her community.

I'll never know for sure because Granny has passed on, but I tend to think that, because her friends had gotten to know me and liked me, they allowed me to be myself. And if Granny had that kind of support system around her—that safety in knowing her friends thought I was okay—she could be okay with my being different, too. I never saw that kind of support system around my mom. I think it makes a big difference when you know that your relationships with your friends aren't threatened because your son is who he is.

When my mom later began a ceramics studio in our garage, I tried so desperately to recreate how I felt in Granny's space. I was in my early teens by then, and just like at Granny's, the community ladies would all come over and giggle and tell stories. I wanted so badly to be a part of their group. Although Mom never said, "You can't do this," or "You can't do that," I didn't feel the same level of permission to be myself that Granny had given me in her studio. Maybe it was because I was older and no longer a cute little boy. Whatever the reason, there were certain rules of engagement in my mom's studio that I didn't have at Granny's, even if they were unspoken.

I don't know that my mom would have prevented me from helping someone with something artistic and creative, but I felt I had to behave more on the masculine side in the studio. I understood that I could put things in kilns and do the electrical work; women would make ceramic lamps, and I'd help them attach the bar and the lampshade and run the electric cables, which Mom had taught me how to do. That task was seen as more of a "man thing," so it seemed more acceptable. When I wasn't doing those things, I felt like I was being sent away. My mom would tell me that I had to go inside and do chores—get dinner ready or do the laundry (which, ironically, are considered to be more female chores).

"But I want to be here," I would argue. *I'm supposed to be here*, I thought. I kept trying to insert myself into something that was interesting and exciting; my brother had cars to work on and machines to build, but where could I go? I don't know what was going on in my mom's mind. I sensed that her focus was on other things—like making ends meet, making sure we had clothes, food, and a roof over our heads. Granny, on the other hand, wasn't worried about money; she was more worried about keeping her place neat and tidy.

Fortunately, my stepmom gave me another outlet for creativity and an opportunity to be myself. She helped me with making macramé. One year, I made macramé hangers as gifts for everyone, to hold ceramic pots from Mom or Granny's studio. I also learned from my stepmom how to use a loom and stitch together little hot pads. She loved and supported my art. Still, those spurts seemed to disintegrate as soon as I stepped outside the safety of home. Even at home sometimes, my cousins would make fun of me. My Aunt Linda, who was my mother's sister, didn't know what to do with me or how to treat me, but interestingly, her husband—my Uncle Dan—would stand up for me. Uncle Dan came from a very large family with lots of siblings with kids, and not all of them were nice. One day, Uncle Dan must have overheard them tease me.

"Everyone into the living room!" he ordered. "You all need to be respectful. Don't be saying things about your cousin Tracy." I almost couldn't believe it. I looked up at him with such gratitude that an adult man was sticking up for me. It felt special to have a "masculine" adult treat me with such respect. Essentially, my hypermasculine farmer uncle gave me permission in that moment to be me! While the shame had already set in from my cousins taunting me, I felt I was seen by Uncle Dan. His words to the group of kids resonated with me, communicating that I mattered and it was okay to be me.

With most of the male figures in my life, it felt like I only received half their love; it wasn't fully realized. They didn't know what to do with me. Grandpa had a big train set in his room; if I wanted to play with my grandfather, I had to play with trains. I enjoyed it, but not in the way my brother did. Rick was the mechanically minded one who liked to build things, so he and Grandpa had a bond that I could not penetrate. There were constant little reminders that I wasn't "normal." I tried my best to not be feminine. I tried working on cars, and I tried painting model cars with my dad. I tried hunting. But I just thought, *Oh my God, this is so boring and ridiculous.* It took so much effort to be someone I was not, in order to get people to be okay with me. I felt like I was not enough. Over time, this feeling truly impacted my life decisions as I became desperate to be enough.

There was one day, however, when I learned it was possible to be me *and* be enough. I was in fifth grade. My Lutheran elementary school was putting on a Christmas program, which was to include a choir performance. I was rehearsing "Silent Night" with all the kids in my music class when my teacher said, "Tracy, will you sing the second verse?"

I didn't know why he was asking me this, but I did as I was told, in front of everyone. After class, he called me over and said, "I would like you to do a solo during the program." I was taken aback.

"Me? Are you sure?" I wasn't from a musical family by any means. We didn't have any instruments in the house, and no one sang. And given that money was tight, music lessons were never in the picture. But my teacher saw something in me that I did not.

"Yes. You have such a great range and a very nice voice," he said. I don't remember receiving a lot of compliments in my childhood, so his words surprised me.

"Sure, okay." I agreed to sing in the program.

Fast-forward to the night of the concert, which was held at my Granny and Grandpa's former church, where they raised their daughters. The church sat between 150 and 200 people and felt huge to me. Everyone started filling in as the choir, all of us dressed up, sat in the front row. As the preacher gave a sermon, I was nervous and anxious, waiting for our turn to get on stage. We took our positions, with me in the center front, and started singing the first verse. Then, it was time for the second verse. I stepped forward for my solo, while the other kids hummed the verse. My voice cracked a little, but overall, I did alright. Once the nerves wore off, I loved the feeling of being on a stage! We finished the third verse together, and then *boom*—the room erupted in applause. The feeling was incredible.

It was the applause that got me. And the fact that Granny and Grandpa were so proud. Grandpa even gave me a hug and a twenty-dollar bill. While Grandpa gave us hugs, this felt different; it lingered and it was a strong hug. I could feel how proud he was of me. I'll never forget that moment! My mom hugged me, too, and so did many others—Granny, my cousin, my aunt and uncle, and friends of my grandparents whom I didn't even know. I got acceptance from my family and the community at large. I felt *seen* by them for the very first time in my life.

And then that feeling went away.

I think I've spent the rest of my life trying to recapture it.

It wasn't long after that experience that I saw a college cheerleading competition on ABC with male cheerleaders. They were at Disney World, stunting and running around. *Oh my God*, I thought. It was a stage! It was fabulous. I knew with certainty: *I want to do that.* Pursuing singing didn't feel like an option for me; I knew my family couldn't afford lessons. A lot of singers get their start in the church, but we didn't go to church, so I wasn't part of a choir. *But cheerleading*, I thought, *I can teach myself!*

While other boys were lusting over *Playboy* magazine, I was lusting over the *Varsity* cheerleading catalog. While I'm no longer lusting over it, it was meaningful enough that I still have it today. There was no internet at the time, so I had to order the catalog over the phone. When I looked at the pictures, I thought, *That feels like me. Other boys are doing it, so it has to be okay.* Those boys weren't around small-town Ohio, but they were in the world, which I found validating.

Until seventh grade, I went to a Lutheran school in the middle of nowhere, where my mom and aunt had gone to school. There were only two classrooms: one for kindergarten through fourth grade and one for fifth through eighth grades. Imagine how few kids lived in the area! Yet, there was a boy there who would taunt, tease, and bully me to the nth degree. He would push me, throw stuff at me, call me "faggot" and "sissy," and trip me on the stairs. I didn't even know what faggot meant. There was no Google back then for me to look these words up.

My defense mechanism was to try to ignore him and pretend it wasn't happening. I never fought back, which made me an easy target. Our teacher tried to put him in his place, but that only went so far—the teacher wasn't always around. By the time I completed sixth grade, I couldn't take it anymore. I begged and begged my mother to let me transfer to the new junior high school that had just been built next to Fairbanks High School, and she finally relented.

The best part about the new junior high was that they had a cheerleading team! The Lutheran school had no sports teams. I begged my mother to allow me to try out for the eighth-grade team (tryouts were held the year prior), but she wouldn't budge on that issue. "No, you can't do that. You just can't," she said.

"But why not?" I asked.

"Because you can't. It's too dangerous. They're going to make fun of you." I didn't agree. I had a passion burning inside me, and nothing was going to get in my way. I had a very defiant attitude and still do to this day. That defiant nature is something that I used to think was a bad thing, but I now understand when harnessed for good, it can be a great attribute. It has the ability to help me achieve things no one thought possible.

"You're not going to tell me I can't do what I want to do!" I fought back. I wanted it so badly. I was going to do anything and everything I could to be in that *Varsity* catalog. So, I forged my mom's signature in order to try out.

Tryouts were held in the school gym. I wore my physical education clothing—shorts and a T-shirt. The whole day leading up to tryouts, I was so excited. My dream was *this* close to coming true! I had been given a list of moves and cheers to expect. I already had them down from practicing with neighborhood girls who were younger than I was and who thought cheerleading with an older boy was pretty cool. We would meet in the yard underneath a tree and cheer our hearts out.

I took a deep breath as I stood in line outside the gym with all the other girls. *You've got this*, I told myself. I felt alone in my efforts, though. No one talked to me. I had the feeling the girls were kind of miffed by my presence, as if I were trying to take their spot. Finally, I was called into the gym. At the base of the wooden bleachers was a long table where three adults sat, ready to decide my fate.

"Okay, let's see what you can do," one of them said. I did the first cheer and knew that I'd nailed it. Then, I had to return to the hallway and wait until they called me back as part of a group cheer, so they could see if we stayed synchronized. I felt the group cheer went well, and then we all went back to the hallway to await the results. One by one, they called out the names of the students who had made the team. I waited…and waited…until the final name was called. It wasn't mine. *I didn't make the team.*

I was devastated. I had been so confident that I would make the team. *I'm better than any of those girls*, I thought. I could feel in my soul that this was what I was supposed to be doing; during tryouts, I was on that floor, ready to be seen. I had never been a confident kid; I felt like an oddball and differ-ent most of the time. But for whatever reason, when the doors shut and those women were watching me, it was like theater. I was on. It was a nerve-racking thing for a seventh-grade kid to be doing, but my nerves paled next to my excitement and joy. Until my name wasn't called.

How can they not see how good I am at this? I tried to make sense of it all. *I guess I just need to try harder*, I reasoned. *I can do even better.* It didn't occur to me that I hadn't made the team because I was a boy. Like my family, the judges didn't know what to do with me. I would love to have been a fly on the wall so I could hear what those three women were saying. *We can't put him on the team. He's a boy.* It might have been a safety issue for them, too. Maybe they were worried about me. I'll give them the benefit of the doubt that it wasn't malicious. They could have forbidden me from even trying out; they might have underestimated me and thought I wouldn't be any good, so it was no big deal to let me try out. But I ended up being good, so they had a decision to make that they might not have been expecting. I think the coaches, like my mom, were trying to protect me—along with themselves. The administration didn't know what to do about a male cheerleader either; a lot of people weren't up for that fight in the '70s. There were no rules stating that I couldn't be on the team; back then, it wasn't common for people to try out for sports that weren't typically for their gender. But there were no rules stating that I *could* be on the team, either.

Until cheerleading tryouts, I was relatively innocuous. I was just another kid at the school. After I tried out—despite not making the team—the floodgates opened. Word got out fast...all the way to my brother. Although the doors between the junior high and the high school remained closed, we were both Kinghams. Kids from the junior high who had older siblings at the high school spread the news that Rick's little brother had tried out for cheerleading. He was ashamed and embarrassed; he had to have gotten teased.

"I hate you!" my brother screamed at me after school one day, having stomped up the stairs and into our bedroom. "You're ruining my life!" No one else was home; my mom was driving a school bus, and Tom was working second shift. I was in shock because until then, my brother and I had been close. Clearly, he was getting pushback from his peers about his "weird little brother." Rick played football and was a track star, and most members of the school were in the FFA—Future Farmers of America. It wasn't the kind of crowd to welcome a male cheerleader.

After Rick's heated announcement, he stormed out of the house and drove off to his girlfriend's place. Alone, I sat and cried profusely. Suicidal thoughts began to enter my mind. *If I can't be me, then what's the point of living?* My own brother hated me, and—even though it was probably out of safety and caring—my mother wouldn't let me try out, which reemphasized the message that it was not okay to be myself and I had to continue to hide. Despair took over, until I remembered what I'd seen on TV. I had proof that I wasn't alone. *Other guys are cheerleaders. Why can't I do it, too?*

Back at school, the taunting, teasing, and bullying ramped up. Just like at the Lutheran school, one kid in particular was off-the-charts cruel. He would verbally and physically abuse me, tripping me as I went down the hall. My mom visited the school office many times regarding that kid, but he wouldn't stop. Looking back, he was effeminate, too; his acting out may have been to cover up his own denial.

I don't recall having school friends or any sort of connections that most people would associate with high school. I think the bullying overshadowed any friendships. There were a couple boys who I got along well with, but they wouldn't stay in my life long. I was in Boy Scouts in junior high school and had a good friend—I'll call him "Liam"—who I was attracted to without yet realizing it to be in a sexual way. He was one of the few boys who was nice to me. He'd defend me when kids would tease or bully me. He was bigger, so other kids wouldn't mess with him. Looking back, aligning myself with him may have been a survival instinct. But when I started to reveal more of myself to him and then tried out for cheerleading, even he backed away for fear of retaliation or being guilty by association. He didn't want to be seen as gay.

I always gravitated toward girls, but I didn't have a lot of friendships with them because they would turn on me; they'd take information and give it straight to the boys, who would then use it against me. The girls who had liked me stopped associating with me at the same time as the boys; otherwise, they'd be taunted and teased as well. It was all about self-preservation. This dynamic started my delicate dance of reveal and assess, reveal and assess. *Okay, I feel safe. I can reveal more.* I was never able to just announce, "This is me!" like I felt hetero kids were able to do. Looking back, though, I wouldn't change the fact that I tried out for cheerleading, despite it having ruined my social life. I did exactly what I was supposed to do.

CHAPTER 3:

Dangerous to Be Different

After I didn't make the cheerleading team for eighth grade, I committed to making it the following year. I couldn't get the images of the cheerleading competition television show and cheer uniform magazine out of my mind. I'd have to try out in the spring of my eighth-grade year to make the Fairbanks High School team my freshman year.

Once again, I gathered up a few of the neighborhood girls from Unionville Center and practiced under the big tree in our yard. I taught the girls the motions and cheers that I knew to expect from tryouts, testing our formations and making sure we were synchronized. We'd be out there all day. A girl named Audrey, who was a year younger than me, was also trying out for the team, so she was as invested as I was.

I put all my energy into becoming a cheerleader because, despite the fact I didn't make it the first time—and despite the fact that I was being tripped and punched and called a faggot and sissy boy and every derogatory term in the world—I was all in on this dream. I wanted to be on that television show. I wanted to be on that stage at Disney World, running around, smiling, clapping, and tossing the girls up in the air.

This time, my mother knew I was going to try out. Once again, she was not supportive, but I insisted, "I'm doing this. I don't care what you say."

She relented. "It's not going to be easy if you make the team, Tracy," she warned me as she signed the papers.

"It's not easy now," I told her. I don't think my mom realized just how hard school had been for me; I kept a lot to myself. But I was passionate about this path. I was going to keep trying until I got a yes.

Leading up to tryouts, I had the cheers and routines on constant replay in my head. I rehearsed them mentally while riding the bus to school, visualizing my success. I did the same thing while in line for my turn in front of the judges at the school gym. This time, there were different judges. The cheerleading advisor from the year before was no longer there. The high school basketball coach became the interim cheerleading coach until they could find a female teacher who would agree to coach the team.

Once again, I did my solo routine, followed by a group routine. And again, I felt I nailed both routines. Just after tryouts, the judges announced the results. They began reading off names for each team. I held my breath until the final position on the team was shared...

"...and Tracy Kingham."

I couldn't believe it! I had done it! Someone had given me a chance!

I don't know what made this coach different; he was the school civics teacher and the basketball coach. Perhaps he was more familiar with collegiate cheerleaders at Ohio State University in Columbus. There had been male cheerleaders there since the 1950s—which is ironic, because our community was less than an hour from Ohio State. Whatever the reason, I knew I was good, and he saw it, too. That doesn't mean he was happy about it, though. Before I had time to celebrate my name being on the roster, he came over to me and said, "Well, son, you made it. So, what are you going to do? Wear a skirt?"

"No," I replied. I pulled out my *Varsity* catalog, which I carried with me all the time, and showed it to him. "They make pants for boys. I'm going to order a pair of pants." The team had a meeting where we decided on uniforms—they would have the image of a panther sitting on a megaphone. I thought that was so cool! It was thrilling getting the cheerleading pants in the mail, sewing on the patch, and seeing my name stitched on them. I felt as if I had arrived; I was fulfilling my dream. I do have memories of my mom helping me to sew the patch on the sweater. She could do anything, I remember thinking. I'm not sure what was on her mind, but in that moment, I felt close to her. All summer, I couldn't wait for school to start so I could wear my sweater on game days!

I had to get a different sweater from the one they ordered for me, though, because I was so tiny. Around that time, my mom had even taken me to the doctor and asked, "Why is he not in puberty?" Many boys at the school were getting mustaches and showing chest hair above their shirt line. I didn't even have hair under my arms. I didn't have a growth spurt until I left high school. In hindsight, this may have been because I felt more freedom to relax and be who I was by then. At eighteen, I woke up in the middle of the night with intense leg pain and seemingly overnight grew to the six feet, two inches that I am today!

It was exhilarating making the high school cheer-leading team. I'm not going to say cheerleading saved me. But cheerleading revealed to me that I have the ability to do anything I set my mind to. I don't know if I'd be here today if it hadn't been for cheerleading. There were so many times in my adult life when I used cheerleading as a source of my own strength and determination, often thinking, *If I could make the cheerleading team despite all of the barriers, I can do anything I set my mind to.*

My joy was curtailed, however, before that school year started. We had cheerleading camp for a week in August at the Universal Cheerleaders Association (UCA) Camp in Kentucky. They had to put me in a different dorm because I was a boy and couldn't be in the girls' dorm—another reminder that I was different. I was part of the group when the coaches pulled us together, but when we weren't cheering, I was by myself. I even ate by myself. The girls were not nice. Despite having boys on their squads in college, I remember the UCA instructors not being kind, either, which baffled me. Of course at age fourteen, I took this to mean that something was wrong with me.

They hired a new coach over the summer—a young, petite woman who wasn't very helpful. I was used as the center of the squad for balance, because what do you do with a guy who's dressed differently? I didn't use pom-poms, either. I learned from watching the collegiate cheerleading competitions that I needed to behave differently than the girls. I tried to be more masculine, but I'm not sure I was very good at that!

At time-outs during the games, or between quarters, I loved being in the middle of the floor, despite the heckles and jeers. I will never forget the exhilarating feeling of having a megaphone and yelling the cheers. We were synchronized, and the crowd would cheer at the end. For a moment—just a few seconds—I felt like nothing else mattered. It was reminiscent of the applause and adulation I'd experienced after my choir solo. Then, as we'd run off the floor when the time-out was over, there would be some sort of derogatory comment or heckling. My freshman year, games didn't have a big audience— mostly just parents and some friends of those on the team. But I'd hear jeering from some audience members or teams from other schools that would cross through the gymnasium. Other people had to have heard, but nobody—I mean *nobody*—would ever stick up for me or apologize on their behalf, even the adults. It's disgusting to think how adults didn't stick up for kids who were being bullied or called names.

I did have a voice on the squad my freshman year; I was able to share ideas about formation or certain moves. Overall, the girls on the squad were nice to me at that time. I have a fond memory of what we called our "hello" cheer. We'd go over to the opposing team and stand in formation; I was usually in the middle. When I called my name out with a huge smile on my face, "TRACY," and then the audience called back my name as part of the cheer, it was so thrilling. It was a moment when I felt seen.

Outside of those special moments, however, reality set in. My neighbor Audrey, who had practiced with me, made the squad as well. Once she got into high school, she could see that I was treated differently, and our friendship dissolved. The boys at the school were worse, and their worst behavior came out toward the end of my freshman year, after tryouts. I didn't make it onto any squad my sophomore year, again because I was a boy. The hurt and pain of being a cheerleader one year but not the next was very traumatic. It felt like the naysayers, the haters, and the bigots had won. It felt like the entire school was against me being myself. Every time I put myself out there, I was treated so unkindly, and it seemed everyone wanted to push me back into place, but I persevered, kept practicing, and kept trying to reach my goals.

In tryouts the following year, although the teasing didn't subside, it wasn't as rough, because I wasn't thrust into the public each week at a football or basketball game. Nevertheless, I tried out and made the varsity team for my junior year. Nobody cared too much when I was a freshman, but being on varsity meant I had knocked a senior off the team, which caused all hell to break loose. The parents called a board meeting to discuss kicking me off the team. My mom attended the meeting. I remember feeling so deflated—yet again, another defeat. I had worked so hard. The hurt and the damage of that situation persisted well into my adulthood, in the form of fear of being ostracized for being myself. To this day, the fear of putting myself out there when I do something new causes me to stop and think. In some cases, I freeze and won't move forward. I always have to remind myself that the pain is from my youth and that it's going to be okay.

There were no rules prohibiting male cheerleaders from participating. I had made the team fair and square. Mom came home and told me, "You're fine— you are still on the squad." Now that she'd gotten used to the idea of me being on the team and saw how badly I wanted it, she thought it was ridiculous how intent they were on getting me removed from the squad. But being on the squad didn't feel like a victory. I felt like the whole community was against me; it wasn't just the kids at school, but the parents, too. Years later, I found out from my friend Melissa, who was my cheerleading partner in college, that she'd had a nearly identical experience. She made varsity as a freshman, kicking a girl out of her spot; that girl's parents went to the board and tried to get her removed. Despite some people's efforts, I didn't get kicked off the team. I remember thinking, *Okay. I do have a spot here.* It was a bit of a relief that they allowed me to stay on. But that's when things became really intense in the life of Tracy Kingham.

The boyfriend of the girl I had "knocked off" the team was a burly football player. I can still see him today, towering over me. In my memories, he's at least seven feet tall. Keep in mind, I still hadn't had my growth spurt. Right after the team announcement was made over the loudspeaker, he came over to my locker, slammed the locker door shut, and got up in my face.

"I'm going to kill you, motherf—r," he said. He didn't touch me, but I got the message. I'm sure it was a scare tactic to get me to quit. His girlfriend was distraught. From his perspective, she didn't make the squad and this little faggot did. He was trying to protect his woman. I knew I was in trouble, and I lived in utter fear from that day forward. My locker that year was across from the lunch area, in between the gym doors. It was a little bit like no-man's- land, away from the classrooms where teachers would be coming and going. This meant that kids felt like they could get away with whatever they wanted. As a result, visits to my locker were risky business. I learned very quickly how to navigate space and stay safe. I tried my best not to be found alone; when the bell rang after each class, I'd hang around the classroom as long as I could before making a run for it to my next class. I leaned on other kids who were considered "outcasts." We stayed by each other when we could, although I wasn't really friends with any of them. Gym locker rooms were frightening for me. I never showered at school. I was first in, first out. I learned to navigate the school day by sitting in the entryway of the school during lunch or while waiting for my mom to pick me up. It was near the office, and there were always kids and teachers around, so it was my safe zone.

The biggest bully of them all was a guy I will call Richard Kipman. Because my last name begins with K-I-N and his with K-I-P, his locker was next to mine. He'd slam my locker and push me whenever I was next to him, which was every day. He would not allow me to get into my locker, and when I did, sometimes he would slam the door on my fingers. *If he would just lock me in my locker, I would be better off*, I thought. I didn't want to face the world. Teachers would walk past and witness his behavior—and do absolutely nothing about it. Not only were our lockers next to each other, Richard also sat behind me every morning in homeroom. Without fail, he'd say something derogatory or do something that would make the room laugh at me. He was mean-spirited and awful, and I couldn't get away from him. There was name-calling, as well as pushing and shoving in the hallway between classes, always by the boys. Girls giggled or stayed away from me.

Bullying was a part of both my junior high and high school years. In junior high, it was more about teasing and taunting: "You're a girl. Tracy is a girl's name. You're so gay." My freshman year, the bullying escalated. After I'd made cheerleading my junior year, my locker was broken into and vandalized, with "faggot" written inside. A threatening note was also left, saying something like, "Be careful. You're a disgrace."

I tried to hide the bullying and harassment from my mom. She had warned me it was going to happen, and I didn't want her to know she had been right. I also didn't want to be taken off the cheerleading team. I felt like I was my own parent; I took care of myself because I didn't want the things that I loved to be taken away from me. I felt that if I went to an adult, they would remove me from the team.

In hindsight, I realize how much these events impacted the rest of my life. Here was this thing I loved, cheerleading, that made me come to life. But with it, there was always some battle to wage. I felt I never had permission to realize the full expression of my passion; I always had to protect myself. Those experiences stayed with me as an adult; I never again went after anything fully, because I was afraid it would be taken away from me. Eventually, that fear turned into a self-fulfilling prophecy.

CHAPTER 4:

Hiding from Mr. Collins

I know that teachers saw I was being bullied. My homeroom teachers had to have heard what Richard was saying to me. The coach who had gotten me on the squad knew what was happening. None of them tried to stop it, or if they did, I never saw it. No one ever said anything that would let me know they were watching out for me. Teachers and parents didn't intervene the way they do today, and it was a full two decades before the start of the anti-bullying movement.

The only one who seemed to notice and want to do something about my situation was Mr. Collins, the school guidance counselor. I didn't have much interaction with him in ninth grade. Tenth grade is when he began calling me into his office, saying, "Hey, Tracy, come here." He would check in and ask, "Are you okay?"

"Yeah," I'd say, very stoic. "Of course. I'm fine."

"If you ever need anything, I'm here for you."

"Okay, great."

Someone must have witnessed me going into his office, because then the teasing turned into "You're like Mr. Collins." Mr. Collins was a very thin, tall, older man, probably in his fifties. When kids said I was like him, I thought, *No, I'm not. I'm not old and skinny.* If I'd been paying attention, I would have noticed that his mannerisms were effeminate. He had a creamy white sweater that he always wore or had hanging on his chair. Looking back now as a gay adult male, I can see his clothing was effeminate as well, very tailored and formfitting.

I still didn't know what the words "gay" or "faggot" even meant. By then, I knew I liked boys (because of those cheerleading magazines), but I didn't make the connection that liking boys meant I was gay.

Mr. Collins had an office in the main administration office, with the principal and vice principal's offices nearby. Some of our early conversations were about college guidance, i.e., "What do you think you want to major in? What are you interested in?" Gradually, he asked to see me more often, and the questions started shifting. At one point, as I was sitting in the chair in his office, he said, "I've witnessed what the kids are saying to you. Do you feel that that is you?" I was a little taken aback. In hindsight, he was coaching me to out myself. I thought, *I don't know. Are you thinking I am, too?* but I froze up. He quickly backed off when he saw my reaction. At that time, I was so naive. I knew I was different, but I wasn't sexual yet. I didn't understand what being gay meant, so I didn't actually know enough to hide it and be closeted. I was just trying to survive.

Then, one day, he went from asking a lot of questions to suggesting, "Here, let me give you a hug." At first, that was nice. *Okay, someone cares about me*, I thought. I didn't suspect any malice or ill will in the gesture. After I'd cheerlead at games, he'd be there waiting, wanting to talk to me, and I would. It was very intriguing; I had no relationships or friendships, was afraid to be around boys, and most definitely was afraid of men. Now, here was a man who was nice to me and seemed like he cared. At home, no one wanted to talk to me about feelings. With Mr. Collins, conversations were very caring and focused on my well-being: *How are you doing? Is everything okay? Is there anything that I can do to help you?* It felt very genuine. It felt like, for the first time, someone was actually concerned about Tracy. Again, not to discredit my mom—I know she cared for me deeply—but we did not have conversations like that. It was the '70s, after all. I started to put my trust in Mr. Collins. I don't remember him giving me any real advice; he would always just ask questions and then sit there and listen. It was very comforting. It felt loving.

Then things started to change. I remember one instance where I was leaving a football game wearing my cheerleading outfit, and kids' parents were coming up to me screaming, "You're ruining our community, faggot," and "Get the "f— out of here and leave." I was trying to walk from the game to my mom's car so I could go home, but it became clear that it wasn't safe for me to walk alone anymore. My mom never went to my games, but she'd pick me up afterward. I think that was as much as she was able to support me. It wasn't out of being unloving; I think she was just protecting herself from seeing the hatred that was being thrown at me. I can only imagine some of the things she might have heard about me while driving the school bus. Because we had different last names, nobody would have known that she was my mother, so there was perhaps more open discussion in her presence.

Mr. Collins witnessed the taunting and slurs that day and took a greater interest in me. Soon afterward, I was at school when he invited me into his office again. This time, he turned the blinds down and shut the door. *No big deal*, I thought. We were in the counselor's office, where kids had private conversations. I don't remember what the discussion was about that day, but I know I was very guarded. "I'm a good man," I remember him saying. Then, like he often did, he gave me a hug and I left. He called me back into his office the following week. This went on for months; I realized as an adult, after a good amount of therapy, that he was grooming me. He was trying to establish trust—shutting the door and seeing if I'd stick around, giving me a hug and reading my body language. I'm sure he was assessing my tolerance for his behavior.

Then, one day when I was in class, a staff member knocked on the door and told the teacher, "Tracy's needed in the office." *What did I do? Am I in trouble?* I thought. I grabbed my books and made my way to the office, not sure who wanted to talk to me or why. But when I stepped into the office, no one was there. Usually, the secretary would be at her desk and the principal would be in his office. Today, no one. *What the heck is going on?* I wondered. *Who wanted to see me?*

"Hey, Tracy. Come here—I want to talk to you." Mr. Collins poked his head out of his office. My heart jumped. I didn't want to, but I stepped into his office. He closed the door behind me. And then, I heard a little *click*. He had locked the door. That set off my radar. *Why would he lock the door? Something's not adding up here.* We went into our normal routine of talking: "Tell me about school and your classes. Are you having problems with the kids?" I told him about Richard Kipman. It was always about him. Then he said, "Come here." I approached him, which felt a little strange. Something wasn't like the other times we'd talked; he seemed a bit anxious himself. He stood up and gave me a hug, holding me for what felt like too long. Then he put his hand on my lower back, much closer to my butt. I could feel his heart racing, and the energy wasn't something I had ever encountered from someone else before. I just didn't feel comfortable at all. Then he went a bit further, putting his hand on my butt.

What did he just do?! I froze. I was shocked. *I've got to get out of here* was my next thought.

He must have sensed that I tensed up. My body became rigid, and I stepped back and away. "Okay, I gotta go." I grabbed my bag, unlocked the door, opened it, and left. I never went back to Mr. Collins's office again. Thinking back on it now, I am alarmed by how calculated that whole experience was. He saw a rare opportunity when no other staff was in the office, and he seized it. I'm not sure if anything more would have happened, or if he would have forced me to do something more, then denied any accusations. In most cases back in the early '80s, the adult would have been believed over the student. An educator doing something like this wasn't openly discussed. I'm grateful that I had the instincts to take care of myself and that he didn't push the issue any further.

From that moment on, I did everything I could to avoid him at all costs. I had to "hide" from him. I made up any excuse to never have to go into that room again. I started tracking where he was; if I saw him coming down the hallway, I darted in the other direction. One time, he was outside the office when I passed by. He called me over, saying, "Tracy, come here," and I just walked right past. I came in late to school one day and had to drop off a note from my mom. He heard me and came out of his office. "Tracy, after you're done there, I would like to talk to you for a bit," he said.

"Nope, I've got to go," I replied. I knew what he was doing. He needed to talk to me to make sure I wasn't going to say anything about what had happened in his office. I considered reporting him to school authorities, but I didn't want to open a can of worms. I had no proof of what he'd done, anyway; it would have been my word against his, and I was just a kid. Plus, there was constant questioning in my mind about my role: Was it my fault? The experience scared me, because it stirred up things inside me that I was pushing down and didn't want to be true. Was I like Mr. Collins?

By my senior year, he was gone. I'd love to know why he left. In hindsight, I'm sure I wasn't the only kid he had been inappropriate with. Today, after all these years processing what happened at such a young age, I don't feel guilty saying that I loved the moments I shared with Mr. Collins—until he touched me inappropriately. It felt like I was being seen. But in fact, I was just being used, which is a tough lesson to comprehend at such a young age. To this day, I want to shout to all children suffering from abuse much worse than mine that they didn't do anything wrong and the adult is at fault. It took me a long time to believe that.

I had inner strength that I wasn't fully aware of at the time. I had been a young boy looking for love and acceptance, and here was this male authority figure giving me attention. But I understood it was the wrong kind of attention; I knew I deserved better. I think what gave me the strength to walk away was Granny's love. I didn't want to disappoint her. I also give credit to my mom, my stepmom, and all my grandparents for giving me enough courage to just say "no"; their love gave me a reason to stand up for myself. Their homes gave me a safe haven. I loved going to Granny and Grandpa's to hang out; just watching TV with them was comforting.

That experience with Mr. Collins was the first sexualized experience from a man that I'd had. What I was running from was not necessarily him but myself, because being touched by a man resonated with me. I liked it. I was scared, but also turned on a little bit—not by him, the person, but by the touch of a man. That's when I learned that the adoration I'd had for my friend Liam and for the boys in those magazines were about sex. I wanted to be with a man in that way and have a shared experience with them. And that's when I learned what it meant to be gay.

In hindsight, Mr. Collins's abuse—what I consider grooming—really rocked my world. After that incident, I had no trust left in men. From then on, I inherently thought all men would turn out like Mr. Collins, wanting something from me. The sense of betrayal never left me.

When I would go and see Mr. Collins for our "talks," I'd thought I had this one safe space, but he breached that trust. And there was not a soul I felt I could talk to about it. But I did seek out a safe space, with Jane Brown.

In the summertime, I was always at Jane Brown's house. Jane lived down the street from me. Her daughter Amber and I were friends, but Amber was several years younger than me. I would tell my mom

I was going over to see Amber—and there were times we'd go up to her room and just hang out for a little bit—but mostly, I was there to hang out with Jane. She was divorced; her ex-husband lived down the street in another house. Their divorce had been very contentious, and she had custody of their two kids. Amber's older brother would make a snide remark from time to time when he had friends around, but for the most part, he left me alone. When nobody was around, he was really cool. He, too, was a product of his environment and kept up appearances to keep himself safe. He couldn't empathize with the "gay boy," or others would think *he* was gay. He didn't want to be seen as a gay sympathizer. Similar to my brother, he had to play the part. Jane was a pretty strict disciplinarian, so his behavior was kept in check.

I loved going to Jane's house. Their home was simple and unassuming. I'd come in the back door, into the kitchen. It seemed like Jane was always washing dishes. It got to a point where I would just walk in without knocking; I felt like it was my house. Jane would make lunch, and the three of us—Amber, Jane, and me—would hang out in the living room, watching soap operas like *The Young and the Restless* and *The Bold and the Beautiful*, and whatever came on after that.

That house was my little safe place to go and spend time when the outside world was not being so kind to me, or if I was bored. I have comforting, fond memories of a place where I had permission to be whoever I needed to be. I don't remember talking with Jane about the emotional things I was dealing with at the time, like the stresses of school or bullying. It wasn't a deep relationship, but it was a *safe* relationship. Sadly, she passed away from cancer soon after I went to college.

Looking back, I felt safe with women—not just with Jane Brown, but also women like Granny and all her girlfriends—because they wouldn't breach trust in the same way a male authority figure might... like Mr. Collins did. I love watching *The Golden Girls*, because it brings back amazing memories of being with Granny's friends, able to relax and find sanctuary. I'm lucky to have had that.

CHAPTER 5:
Keeping Up Appearances

I thought about ending my life. Why would I not want to get rid of all the pain? I had access to guns; there was no lock on the gun cabinet. But I wasn't a violent person, and the 1970s wasn't a time when we heard much about guns being used to harm ourselves or others. Guns were for hunting, used to shoot rabbits and deer. There was also no internet. I believe my time in Granny's studio is what saved me from committing self-harm. I had an outlet, however temporary.

At the time, it seemed like everyone around me was ignoring my trauma. I tried to ignore it as well, but the noise was always there. I was someone different at school than at home, where I could—in some ways—take the mask off and relax a bit, or at least dissociate. After the situation with Mr. Collins,

I still had one year left of high school. I went into total survival mode. I didn't try out for cheerleading at the end of my junior year; I just couldn't do it anymore. I was completely exhausted by hiding from Mr. Collins, hiding from Richard Kipman, hiding from a bad situation around every corner. I did everything I could to just get through each day. I couldn't wait to get the hell out of there.

I started hanging out with the wrong crowd—a group of guys who didn't fit in, either, and who resorted to drinking, smoking pot, and skipping school to deal with their pain. I wasn't looking to hang out with people I liked or people who liked me. I was just looking for anyone who *would* hang out with me, period. No one else would speak to me. For whatever reason, these guys let me in; maybe they were using me in some way, just as I was using them. By hanging around them, I could say, "They're my friends...I'm not the kid you think I am." I was still locked into trying to keep the outward appearance of being a straight guy in rural Ohio.

Together, we'd ride bikes through the tiny town center, go down to the creek and fire up a joint, go fishing, or sit around watching TV. I didn't drink—I didn't like the taste of beer—but I'd throw darts with the guys in the garage while they drank. One day, I skipped school with them. I remember that day clearly.

I had it all planned out. My mom was a school bus driver, so she always left early, long before my brother, my sister, and I had to get up and go to school. My sister left first; her school was across the street from our house. Then my brother, who was driving at that point, left to go to the vocational school he was attending before my bus would arrive. It was an easy, "well-thought-out" plan to skip school that day with the boys.

I went frolicking all day, convinced that I'd fooled everybody. However, as I said, my mom was a school bus driver—not mine, but she knew all the other drivers. She was looking for me after school to make sure I put the roast in the oven when I got home. She proceeded to go to my bus, and of course the bus driver informed her that I wasn't on the bus that morning and hadn't been at school that day. I went back home and went to my room. Soon after, I heard a school bus pull into the driveway, brakes slamming and rocks flying.

Oh, shit. Mom's home.

"Tracy Lee Kingham! You get down here right this second!" she called from the kitchen. Not only had I skipped school, I'd also left the roast in the oven. I was grounded. At first, I was just embarrassed that I'd been caught, but after having time to think while stuck in my room, I realized that I was going down a path that wasn't me. I never skipped school again.

There was one thing I did, however, that no one ever found out about. One day, I was sitting around watching TV with the guys when, one by one, they left to go home. Eventually, it was just me and the guy whose house we were at.

"I'm bored. Want to go down to the basement?" he asked. Something felt familiar about the situation...

like he was testing the waters. It reminded me of being with Mr. Collins, except this was a high school kid. I could feel sexual tension in the air, without really having that terminology in my vocabulary yet.

"I'll show you my model cars," he added.

"Okay." I didn't know what else to say.

The only access to the basement was from outside, like the cellar entry in *The Wizard of Oz* movie, and there was a small workshop inside. We went to the workshop, and he showed me the models he was working on. I could feel his excitement at being alone with me. I remember we wrestled a little, which was titillating and super exciting...boys never did anything with me, especially touching.

Nothing much happened that first time, but after about two more visits down there alone, he began to make a very slow pass. *Whoa, what just happened here?!* I thought. We locked eyes, and I could tell he was looking to see what my reaction was. For straight boys and girls, sexual advances are known and understood. Queer individuals, on the other hand, first have to give clues—to say things and wait for a reaction, before moving to something a bit more "obvious." At that time especially, in the '70s in rural Ohio, it was a matter of being safe, not jumping to quick conclusions that could get you hurt—or worse, killed.

Therefore, I was very hesitant at first; rather than feeling excited that there was another male who felt the way I felt about men, I was afraid of the backlash. After it happened, I was nervous that he would tell someone...but he didn't. So, another day we did it again, and it was thrilling—but in the back of my head, I was so worried word would get out. After a couple of times, I got freaked out. *Does this mean I truly am different? I am playing into what people are saying about me.* Until then, I had been denying my sexuality to myself; I really didn't want to believe it. I understood it to be a very terrible thing, and I didn't want to lose everything—my family or my life. If it got out that I was doing sexual things with a boy, it could mean not being able to cheer.

After a handful of experiences with this guy, I stopped hanging out with that crowd. *I'm not doing this anymore*, I decided one day. I think it was out of fear of repercussions. I already had enough to deal with. Regardless, I knew that my liking boys was going to come out someday. When I looked ahead at my future, I wanted a husband; I wanted kids with that husband. *But that won't be possible*, I thought. None of my desires made sense to me. I was trying to figure out who I was, and also trying to prove to myself that I wasn't like Mr. Collins. I either shut down or tried to keep up appearances.

I even sexually explored with girls for a while; there were twins who lived in town and propositioned me, and I said what I knew I was supposed to say: "Okay." I hated every second of being with them and pretending. It was just not me. Since I didn't have access to others who were like me—apart from the one guy I experimented with but wasn't really into—I had to sit and be with who I was.

My exit strategy was to graduate high school and get the hell out of Dodge. I took advantage of a business track offered by the school my senior year, which allowed me to do a half day of classes and a half day of work experience. Since my mom had a business, I convinced her to sign the waiver for me to get work credit. I would go home after lunch to work in her ceramics studio, where she also made other arts and crafts and wholesaled them to stores around the country. She was very talented; she made wood frames, and I helped her pack up orders. I enjoyed working and wanted to graduate and get a job as soon as possible.

To try to fast-track my future, I not only worked part-time for my mom my senior year but also got a part-time job working at Rax Roast Beef, a fast-food place in Dublin. Finally, I graduated early, at the age of seventeen, in June 1984. I don't remember much about the graduation ceremony, aside from wearing a cap and gown and walking across the stage. I do remember it feeling like a happy time; I got presents from everyone in the family.

College was not on my mind; no one in my family had gone to college. The expectation was that I would get a job—and immediately, I was offered a file keeper position at Farmers Insurance in Dublin. They had just opened a new office and needed someone to set up their file systems. I had to get a work permit because I was underage. The week after graduation, I packed up my bright yellow Ford Pinto and drove to my new apartment in Dublin.

I was so excited! Dublin was only half an hour away but felt like another world. Not having everyone in my hometown know everything about what I was doing was a major relief. That's when I started to come into my own a bit. I stepped away from my painful high school years, put them behind me, and started anew.

The job reminded me of being with Grandma Kingham, working from home at her big metal desk in the basement. She used to let us kids play with her typewriter. I would sit down and play "office." I loved typing and learned to be a proficient typist. Little did I know, I was learning how to be a businessperson. I was already typing eighty words per minute and knew my way around numbers and receipts. That experience—and playing shop at the ceramics studio—had helped me get the job at Farmers. To this day, I love entering numbers into online accounting software.

I met some nice women at Farmers. Carla lived in Seattle but would come to Dublin to train the staff. Mandy was another staff member; her husband was the head of the Ohio branch. Carla and Mandy took me under their wing. Mandy had such a cute, bubbly personality. She was probably a former cheerleader. Carla was funny. Both of them were fun—and included me in their fun. One time, we were smoking pot in Mandy's apartment; I disappeared upstairs for a while and then came down in a bra and panties. They giggled and laughed. I wasn't into cross-dressing, but it was a personal test to see what the limits of my self-expression were with them. They gave me an opportunity to be myself and feel like I belonged. I always used to say, "That's so totally awesome," so they got me a big purple T-shirt that said, "Totally awesome." I was finally making friends, and I didn't want them to disappear when they saw who I really was, which had always seemed to happen in the past.

I also got to travel to Seattle for training. One of the female trainers became interested in me. I thought, *Well, okay. I'll try this.* I had been a loner for a long time, and it felt nice to be liked. We began a sexual relationship; it felt uncomfortable and odd, but that's also what made it feel safe and familiar. This woman was in her forties and my coworker; it was a very inappropriate relationship on so many levels. But I maintained appearances for a while because I was still not comfortable with myself and was still looking for who I was. When it got quiet and there was no one around, memories and fears came back that were scary to me—that I was gay. I was working so hard during this time to "fit in" and be "normal" (i.e., straight) so that everyone would love me. It was a very toxic internal dynamic. Being with women was one way to keep up the façade.

After three years at Farmers, when I was about twenty years old, I told the VP of Human Resources that I wanted to be a supervisor. She said, "Unfortunately, in order for you to get into management, you're going to need a degree. You can choose whatever degree you want; just do something you love." They let me apply for a night job; I worked the midnight to 7:00 a.m. shift in the computer room, handling big tapes of data and sending the daily financial and policy data entries to Seattle. For a young'un, it was a fantastic gig.

I started taking classes at Columbus State Community College, while working the graveyard shift. I had a one-bedroom apartment in Dublin with my waterbed and a fish tank, and I had a nice car—a Ford Mustang convertible. I was making really good money. I'd visit Mom sometimes; basically, I'd drive over to say hi and then get the hell out of town again. I often visited Granny, who by then lived in the adjacent community of London.

I still wasn't living a gay lifestyle. I had a girlfriend for about a year who was from Plain City, Ohio. This girlfriend was perfect for me because she didn't want to have sex until she got married. I didn't have to do anything that I wasn't comfortable doing. We got along really well. She was hilarious. I liked her parents, and her parents liked me. I just wanted to be normal. I don't think it was conscious, but I accepted for a time that this was my lot in life— this was how I was supposed to live. I liked boys, but I had to have a girlfriend. I wish I hadn't wasted so much of my early adult life pretending. I wonder how much further ahead I would be if I hadn't had to pretend and could have been my true self from an early age. Even to this day, I have always felt like I'm many years behind in my life.

My relationship was the perfect arrangement... until she started planning the wedding. One day, we were standing around in her mom's kitchen when she brought out a catalog, pointed to a dress, and said, "That's the wedding dress I'm going to get." I thought, *Whoa! Who said anything about getting married?!* I hadn't proposed, and we had never discussed marriage. She just assumed it was the natural next step. I was in shock, but I couldn't say much because her mom was right there. The jig was up; I had to figure out a way to get out of the relationship. For weeks, I agonized over how to do it. Then, I finally got an idea: I lied. I told her I liked her best friend.

"I hate you!" she screamed. It was drama, drama, drama. As expected, her friend decided she hated me too, which was convenient because it got both of them out of my life. I'm not proud of any of this; I was young and stupid. I made a lot of mistakes trying to figure out who I was.

If you are someone who can relate to being bullied or not being able to be who you are—especially for those who are young and more vulnerable—my hope is that my story might encourage you not to make mistakes that are detrimental. I learned from my therapist, Angie Speller, that you'll make some mistakes—we all do. But abusing substances, getting into relationships that will hurt others, or using violence are not the way to go. Try to stay true to who you are and listen to and trust your inner self; we all know when we come across a situation that feels odd and prickly. Listen to that feeling, and get out. Abusing substances numbs our inner intuition; missing or ignoring our intuition leads us down what can be a dangerous path. Trust me—time is on your side. If you can find the ability to stay strong and be patient, there is life after high school. Things will get better. And if you know you need a helping hand, please seek the support of a professional.

CHAPTER 6:
Against All Odds

After earning good grades at Columbus State, I applied and was accepted to The Ohio State University in 1987. I took my colleague's advice and decided to study a subject I loved—I applied to the theater department and got a full-ride scholarship. Still, I had the intention of graduating and becoming a manager at Farmers. I wanted to be the boss and earn a manager's salary.

About two weeks after college started, a friend from theater invited me to a football game. Although I loved to cheer in high school, going to sports as a spectator wasn't my thing. I wasn't a campus-life student; I was a little older than my peers because I had waited a few years to go to college, and I lived off campus while I worked. I took her up on the offer anyway, thinking we'd have time to bond.

We sat in the cheap seats—the student section—which happened to be above where the cheerleaders were. All of a sudden, I remembered the college cheerleading competition. A light bulb went off for me. *Those are the guys who were in the magazine! Those are the guys who were on TV!* Once again, I had an inner calling. *I want to do that!* I found out the name of the coach and approached her one day. I felt shy, but determined.

"Hi, I'm a student here, and I'm interested in learning more about cheerleading," I stated boldly.

"Stop by a practice," she nodded. "We meet at French Field House." French Field House was a big indoor football field with a track and bleachers, and it was open to the public. I had to adjust my work schedule to attend a practice there later that week. I walked in nervously and was amazed by all the acrobatics taking place. It was far different from my high school experience with cheerleading, which revolved mostly around traditional cheers like chants and motions, with no gymnastics, no acrobatics, and very little partnering.

I approached one of the male cheerleaders who looked friendly. "Hi, I'm Trace," I introduced myself. I had recently changed my name, thinking it would be more appropriate for pursuing an acting career.

He reached out his hand, saying, "I'm Kirk." I learned that Kirk, like me, had been the only boy on his high school cheerleading team; He was younger than me, still in high school at Centennial High School in Columbus, but he was always there.

"What's with all the acrobatics here?" I asked. "I never did any of that."

"Oh yeah, we do much more of that in cheerleading now. There's a PE class you can take here for it. It's called Acrosport." The class would even fulfill a requirement that I needed for my degree. Kirk went on to tell me that there was a gymnastics coach named Larry who also led a college cheerleading class on Tuesday and Thursday evenings. "Let's go one night," he suggested. So, we did. I sat and watched in complete awe as all these young men flipped around and tossed girls up in the air, with Larry at the helm. At the end of class, Larry came over to us and said, "So what did you think?"

"This is totally awesome. This is exactly what I need," I answered enthusiastically.

"Okay, so let's test you out. What can you do? You've been a gymnast—can you tumble?"

"I can't do anything. I've never done any of that stuff," I replied.

"Then you'll never make it on the team," he said. "You need to have gymnastics skills. A roundoff, a back handspring, and a back tuck are required." He saw the doubt on my face. "The Ohio State cheerleading program is very rigorous. I'm not going to lie; it's intense." He had been a cheerleader at Ohio State, so he definitely knew.

"Well, I would love to learn," I said.

He repeated, "You'll never make it."

I was starting out at twenty-one years old and six-foot-two. The odds were against me. But I didn't care; I knew what I wanted. I looked him in the eye and said, "Well, what do you care? I'm going to pay you anyway."

His pursed-lip expression said, *This guy has gumption.* He had no comeback because he knew I was right. I was mature enough to know that this was a business transaction for him.

"Well, okay. Let's get you started." We started with stretching; I couldn't even touch my toes. I had never worked out in my life, and being limber...what the heck was that?

Now that I realized cheerleading in college was an option, I was all in. I remembered, *This is what I'm supposed to do.* When someone tells me that I can't do something, I am moved to take bigger actions to ensure that I can. I become resolute, thinking, *You can't take my dream away from me.*

Larry was straight and very attractive. He had to physically touch me to train me, and at first, I didn't know how to process that. He was nothing but professional and treated me no differently from anyone else. For my whole life, I had wanted to be treated like everyone else, so when I finally had that, it was jarring. There were gay cheerleaders all around, and because he was comfortable with himself, he could be comfortable with us. It was my own stuff that made it awkward. I also saw all the other straight boys with gymnastics backgrounds tumbling around, which was a little confusing to me. I had thought only gay boys would be cheerleaders, because that was all I had known in my life up to that point.

When I started with Larry, I had no flexibility. But I worked at it every single day, and Larry saw my motivation and commitment. I was going to do whatever it took. Coincidentally, he opened up his own gym not long after I started working with him, and he allowed me to come in every day without charging me. He saw my passion and the progress I was making. Tuesdays and Thursdays I took his group classes, where I learned tumbling and stunting. I excelled at stunting, throwing the girls in the air, catching them with their feet, and lifting them up. But at my height, tumbling was challenging. Through the years of cheering at this intense college level, I dislocated fingers, hurt my ankle multiple times, and even fractured vertebrae in my back. I had no idea it was injured that badly, so I just iced it and kept going. I was icing parts of my body all the time. But I kept practicing.

What I learned was that physically being able to tumble was one thing; the mental challenge was something entirely different. Had I started younger, I would have developed those muscles and skills before I had the common sense to fear them. As a grown adult, I understood that if I miscalculated a landing, I could end up severely injured or even dead with a broken neck.

Finally, after five months of practicing every day—either in group classes or privately with Larry—tryouts approached. As Larry had told me, I had to be able to do a roundoff, a back handspring, and a back tuck to make the team. I couldn't even do a back handspring. I was strong, but building flexibility from scratch takes a long time to develop—along with the ability to propel myself backward at six-foot-two, which nobody thought I'd be able to do. I remember Larry muttering,

"I can't believe you're doing this. I just can't believe you're doing this..." as he watched me try.

Tryouts were very competitive, and without having mastered those basics, I knew I stood no chance. Still, at the end of my freshman year at Ohio State, Larry insisted that I try out for sophomore year. "You're not going to make it," he said, "but I want you to know what it's going to take to make it." It was a brilliant strategy for me to get comfortable in front of people and know what I would be up against the following year.

Tryouts were held at French Field House. It was packed with people—family, friends, high school and college students, and school officials. Judges lined tables at the base of the bleachers. It was nerve-racking; it was one thing to practice in a small gym with a few people around, and an entirely different experience to perform for judges on a massive football field.

First, we had to fill out a competition form and put a number on the bottom of our red T-shirts. Then, we had to pair up with the stunting partner we'd selected a week prior. The existing squad had come up with routines that we were given to practice a week before tryouts. I had found a short, stocky, and super sweet senior girl named Vicky who agreed to stunt with me. I was able to toss her like nobody's business. Stunting, or Acrosport, was easy for me; I picked up those skills quickly, and I was very confident tossing girls.

Despite knowing that my motions and rhythm were solid and my stunting skills were strong, I walked into tryouts with zero confidence. I was scared to tumble.

I was most afraid of hurting myself, but also embarrassed because I knew I couldn't do the requirements. My palms were drenched as I paired up with my partner to stunt in front of the judges. I thought, *I just hope I don't drop her!* I had already seen other competitors drop their partners, probably due to nerves. I had strong stunting skills, however, and we got through that part just fine. But next was tumbling.

I took a deep breath in the corner of the floor and ran...launching into a roundoff, back...jump. I didn't do the handspring. I was too much in my head. I had done back handsprings in practice, but not consistently, and on a spring floor; here, I was on turf—there's no spring in turf. I did do a standing back handspring, though...horribly, but I did it. I could do a standing back tuck successfully; that was probably the easiest move for me because I had height. Still, I remember being surprised when I made it all the way around. I looked down at my feet on the ground and thought, *Oh my god, I landed!*

Then I had to go through all the other cheer elements. The girls had to do a bit more dancing, but guys would run around and present ourselves like we were at a game; they even gave us megaphones.

As predicted, that first year I didn't make the team. The next year, I knew what to expect. I had been working with Larry for two years. My tumbling wasn't beautiful, but it was functional. This time, I could do the basic requirements. My stunting was still strong and my motions fabulous. I felt pretty good about my performance but knew selection was highly competitive. At the end of the tryouts, the coach announced the six couples who had made the team. I was crushed—my name was not called. I was so close to giving up at that point. I had worked so hard, and I didn't know if I could keep that effort up; I was working full-time, in school full-time, and practicing full-time.

A week later, the cheerleading coach, Judy Bunting, left a message on my answering machine: "Hi, Trace, I just wanted to let you know I was able to expand the team to eight, in order to cover all the team sports this year. Would you want to be on the squad?" I couldn't believe it! I played the voicemail back multiple times, then called her back. She explained what had happened; it was easier to break the squad into groups of four for all the sports we were cheering for: football, basketball, volleyball, women's sports, and some baseball tournaments. "So, are you in?" she asked.

"Yes!" Of course, I didn't even have to think about it.

We discussed the practice schedule, and she told me to show up the next day. The six other couples had already been practicing. I sat for such a long time after the call, not sure how to react. My heart filled with so much joy. *I really did it*, I thought to myself. I was number eight, but I didn't care that I was the last position on the team. I had made it!

Once again, it was a man who had given me my dream of cheerleading. Larry really took me under his wing, allowing me the privilege of making my dream a reality. I think what made him—along with my eighth-grade male cheerleading coach—so supportive was the fact that they weren't macho men.

They were comfortable with themselves and didn't exude any toxic masculinity that is still a part of our culture today. They allowed for something else to take shape—which was seeing me as an individual rather than a marginalized label. Despite being bullied—and a lot of people and situations that made life as a gay man in the Midwest unbearable at times—there were angels out there, people who didn't fall into the trap of doing what society dictated a man "should" do.

I loved being part of a team with other men. I had never had that experience before. In high school, my female teammates had been mean. This team wasn't perfect—there were some sorority girls on the team who weren't nice—but it was much better than high school. Even though we were a part of a larger team, though, there was segmentation or labels placed on each of us. I remember Sandra, a bubbly, nerdy girl who made the cheerleading squad. And there was a jock girl. The sorority girls were pleasant to my face but then would say mean things about me behind my back. They were ashamed that I was so effeminate. The other gay boys were a bit more closeted or not so up front with their sexuality.

There were times when it felt very similar to high school. I was there, taking up space. The team accepted my being there, but I didn't feel equal. I didn't feel fully appreciated for who I was and what I brought to the team. Looking back now, I realize that was my insecure self buying into the narrative that was given to me during my junior and high school years. I had a constant "you're not worthy" loop playing in my head. Nonetheless, it was real at the time and I so wish I would have really allowed myself the privilege to enjoy every moment. Maybe it was just in my head, but I started to feel like an add-on, since the team had originally only had six members. However, I had what was considered the privilege of being partnered with the team captain, Paula, who was a junior and one of the sorority girls, since we were the tallest members of the team. I stood up front with her while she led us through warm-ups and ran each practice, which was her role as captain.

I learned to navigate the cheer landscape. I confronted them after practice one day and asked them if it was true. "Did you tell people this?" They were dismissive, neither admitting nor denying it. I had a come-to-Jesus moment with a member of the squad where I finally stood my ground. I had heard a rumor that they had said they wished I wasn't on the team because I brought shame to the squad. It may have been because I was in a gay relationship and openly gay, or because they didn't believe I had the skill set to be part of the team. Regardless, I needed to do something about it. I confronted her after practice one day and asked her if it was true. "Did you tell people this?" She was dismissive, neither admitting nor denying it. But for me, it felt like a victory as I had finally advocated for myself. I learned that I had a voice and I needed to start using it to demand better treatment. Prior to that moment, I had been timid and fearful, so I was an easy target. When I stood up and demanded respect, I got it. I never heard any more rumors again.

There were hard times, but I kept the competitions I saw on TV as a driving force in my mind. Now, I had the opportunity to be in those competitions as well. First, we had to qualify to go to the competition. We'd work as a team on a routine, record it, and send the video to the cheerleading competition organizer, the Universal Cheerleaders Association, which would score us and then invite us to compete—or not.

There was so much stress on the team because Ohio State always fared really well in the competition. They had even won nationals a couple years before, so there was an expectation that we had to do well again. Paula was an amazing dancer, as was my buddy Kirk, so the two of them choreographed the routine. We practiced every day of the week and sometimes on weekends, twice a day, mornings and evenings before and after classes. Ten to twelve hours a week were dedicated to practicing. I was also working the graveyard shift from midnight to 7:00 a.m. It was a very daunting existence, but I loved it; it was the realization of the dream that had started when I was watching television at twelve years old, wishing I could be on that stage!

Once we knew we were going to nationals, the intensity really ramped up because we had to do a complete routine. The intensity was because of my mind; I was still struggling with all the synchronized tricks we had to do. They were throwing things at me that were pushing my stress level to peaks I hadn't known. Plus, I had a fear of falling off the stage. I had to do a lot of mental preparation, working on believing in myself. I'd tell myself, "I can do this. I am going to be okay." Because I was learning acrobatics so late in life, the mental learning curve was exhausting. I have a picture of me in my full cheerleading uniform sleeping in a chair between appearances that underscores just how exhausting it was for me. It was pushing my gymnastics to levels I'd never reached before. But I was finally going to compete in that same competition I'd seen on TV!

The competition was held at SeaWorld in San Antonio, Texas. We flew in and checked into our hotel, with all of us sharing rooms. I don't remember who my roommate was, but I remember going from room to room, staying up late and having a good time. We got there a couple of days early, so we had time to go downtown and visit the River Walk, all dressed up in our uniforms; we had to do a couple of appearances for alumni groups in the area.

Then, finally, we got to SeaWorld. I remember going through the gate as a group, finding the outdoor amphitheater where the competition would be held, and walking inside. The stage was so beautiful! *Oh my god, I'm actually here!* I thought. It was just like on TV. It felt like a really big deal to be able to be there...and I still think it is, to this day.

We found our team's section and took our seats on the bleachers. Rehearsals were first, so we were able to watch the other teams practice their routines and see what we might be up against. Then it was our turn on the floor. I'd never been on that floor before, and it was a lot to take in—especially the area where it dropped off. The fear of falling off the stage began to overwhelm me. I messed up a lot during that practice, because I was so worried about taking the team down. My back was still injured, too, which may have contributed to my tendency to go in a crooked line when tumbling.

Then it was time to compete. I took a deep breath, and we were off. Much of what happened next was a blur; everything happened so fast. The whole routine was only a few minutes long, and there were so many tricks and moves happening up and down and all around that I barely had time to think about them. I relied completely on muscle memory. We didn't make it to the television program, they just aired a "shout out" segment of our routine, because our sign was upside down and one of the squad fell at the end of the program. No team is going to win a national title when that kind of thing happens. But I gave everything that I had, despite being scared to death and struggling in some moments; I had to stay in perfect lines next to people tumbling. It wasn't like at the football games where we had plenty of space and could tumble off to the sides; we were now confined to staying within a specific square. If we went out, points were deducted. I put so much pressure on myself because I saw myself as the weakest member of the team. But I didn't mess up; I didn't knock anyone off balance or run into anybody. I delivered. It was the two girls who were not so nice to me who fell. Karma, I guess.

As we got off the floor, everyone was clapping for us. I saw myself as that little boy watching the show on TV, and everything I'd been through felt worth it. The competition was aired on ESPN, making me a minor celebrity in my community (i.e., "Ohio State cheerleader, Trace Kingham"). There were articles about me in the Marysville newspaper. That positive attention didn't erase what I'd been through to get there or take away the pain, but it validated it. I had proven something. *You guys were wrong. See, I was supposed to be a cheerleader. This is who I am. You tried to keep this from me in high school, but now look at me in college!*

I don't know how my mom felt about it. She didn't come to any games at Ohio State that I can recall. My grandparents, however, were thrilled. Grandma and Grandpa Kingham were huge Ohio State fans and came to all the basketball and football games. They were always looking for me on television, and the next time we got together, they'd say, "We saw you on TV!" After one of the games, I hung around and waited for them to come down and have a photo taken on the floor together. It felt so fulfilling to be able to share who I was with them.

It wasn't always easy, but college was much more fun for me than junior high and high school. College is when I became fully realized as a gay man. I was a cheerleader. I had a full-time job. I had an apartment. I even had a boyfriend.

CHAPTER 7:

Coming Out and Going Out

"This is not a place you ever want to find yourself alone," my friend warned. "You have to be alert even walking from the parking lot to the door," another friend chimed in.

Where are they taking me? I thought nervously. "What did you say the name of this place is again?"

"It's called *The Garage*. But first we have to walk through a bar named *Trends* to get there."

I looked at the building we had just parked in front of and were now walking toward. It had no sign. It was just an unassuming, nondescript building in a seedy area of downtown Columbus, Ohio. "Are you sure this is the right place?"

"Yes, we're sure. We come here all the time. Relax. It will be fun."

They couldn't possibly have heard my heart pounding. I had a very skewed version of what it meant to be gay; the belief that gay people preyed on young boys had been formed from my own, narrow, life experience.

We opened the door and stepped inside. It had been dark outside, but this place was *bright*. It was hard to see with all the lights that seemed to be aimed at our eyes. *This is it?* I thought, glancing around the smoke-filled room. I took off my coat and left it at the coat check, revealing my go-to, "going-out" outfit: white T-shirt, tight jeans with a black belt, white socks, and black construction boots. It was the '80s, after all.

There weren't many people inside, just a few older men seated at the bar who today might be called daddies, wolves, or bears. My first impression? It was scary. I wanted to turn around and go right back out the double doors. I had all sorts of thoughts running through my mind, things I had always heard about gay men growing up. *They were predators. They were bad, wrong, evil.* I knew *I* wasn't that way. Now for the first time, here I was, and I was frightened. *Is this a place I have to go to be with others like me?* Was I really allowing myself to be me? I had a nervous stomach and a sickening feeling, which, to this day, is my body's reaction to feeling unsure or fearful of the unknown. In hindsight, I realize I felt the guys were predators. It was an unfair assessment, but my history with Mr. Collins and other older men hadn't been pleasant. While it's most likely that they were not predators, the homophobia I experienced in my upbringing gave me a bias that gay men weren't normal and couldn't be trusted—and to stay away from them. I was implicitly taught as a child that *they will only want to get into your pants*. And then struggling myself as a gay man only made it harder. That night, my first instinct was to protect myself. It was scary. I'm so grateful that I had a solid group of friends who sensed my fearfulness, yet kept assuring me it would be okay. Finding my college friend, and having just that one person to confide in, made all the difference for me to navigate the "new" world of being a gay man.

"It's back there," my friend said, guiding me past the bar and through a set of doors to...the place of my dreams. The room was packed with men *my age* dancing with *other men*. Dance music blared through large speakers...a stage was set for performances...lights were everywhere...a huge mirror on the back wall gave the illusion that the place was even bigger than it was...high-top tables for drinks and mingling were scattered about...small platforms to dance on were all around...and a large dance floor was in the center of it all with *so many men*.

Now I knew what the song by The Weather Girls was all about! I saw guys who looked like me, and at that moment, I began to relax and enjoy myself. My buddy turned to me and said, "I told you that you'd like this place!"

I hadn't known gay bars like this existed until that very moment. In rural Ohio, bars were dark and filled with men drinking, with little room for anything else.

But this was exhilarating; Madonna's music was playing—it was a party, a celebration that I had never experienced before. A place where I could relax for a while and not worry about what the world thought of me. For a moment in time, I felt normal.

Now, I realized there were other meanings of gay, other definitions of what it was to be me. At the bar, men were holding, dancing with, and kissing other men without trying to hide who they were! It was all so new, so liberating. I remember that feeling of utter joy...to think that there was a packed room of people dancing and smiling who were just like me!

It's raining men, amen.

That Saturday night in 1988 hit me like a brick. *I am no longer alone. I can finally be myself!*

Little did I realize, it would take a lot more than one night to break through the shame of my childhood to fully realize my true self.

Throughout college, I was working full-time, cheerleading, and taking theater classes part-time. Because my cheerleading schedule was so demanding, I had to switch my major from a BA in theater to a BA in fine arts with a major in theater, which was a less intensive track. I'd still have to be in performances, but not as many were required.

I wanted to be on stage; I wanted to act. But to stay in the program, I had to reaudition every quarter. After a monologue I gave when going into the final quarter of my first year, a teacher named Joy said to me, "I don't think acting is for you. You should just stick to modeling." Yet again, I was being told—in a room full of professors—that there was something I wanted to do but couldn't. I couldn't be who I wanted to be. It was painful. I liked theater; I really thought I was good at it. The professor could have said, "Choose which path you want to dedicate yourself to," instead of directing me away from theater. I didn't even see myself as attractive enough to model. I had theater teachers say, "How come you don't stand with your chest held high? You're a beautiful person." What went through my mind was: *Well, I just went through hell.*

I don't remember what my response to Joy was, but I stayed in the BFA program the next year, so they clearly didn't kick me out. It messed with my psyche, however, to be told I wasn't good enough. I internalized that message; it's something I've had to learn to overcome and am still learning to overcome. At that moment, I was still looking for external permission to live my life the way I wanted. In a way, I still felt like a little boy, seeking approval. *Why is everyone not seeing me?* I thought. *I know I can do this.*

I met some really nice people while in theater, however, some of whom introduced me to The Garage. I knew there were a couple of gay people in my theater classes—I mean, they were taking me to a gay bar, after all—but we had never actually talked about the fact that we were gay. In the '80s in Columbus, places like The Garage fueled the movement toward greater LGBT acceptance and visibility. I was naive and had no idea how to navigate the world of gay men—all of whom were struggling to break through their pain, anger, and family issues from wanting to be seen.

***

Several months after I started going to The Garage, while a junior in college, I met John. Our eyes met from opposite ends of the dance floor, and we made a connection. I was instantly attracted to him, with his dark, curly hair and white T-shirt. He was a little shorter than me and stocky—very built. I could tell that he took good care of himself. More than anything, though, I could feel his confidence. Looking back, he was probably outwardly too confident, to mask his insecurities.

"Hey, I'm John," he said. "Do you want to dance?"

We danced a bit on the packed dance floor—it was always packed, and the music was always loud. Then he offered to buy me a drink. I accepted and we got to talking, but we couldn't hear each other very well over all the noise. We went our separate ways, with the friends we'd come with, at the end of the night. Then, I saw him again the next weekend. This time, we took our drinks to the outdoor patio, where we were able to hear and get to know each other better. He introduced me to his friends, and I was intrigued.

"We should get together sometime. Outside of here," he suggested.

"Yeah, that would be great."

We exchanged numbers and started hanging out regularly with each other, before transitioning into an official relationship. John was getting his master's degree, while I was getting my bachelor's. We were both busy with classes, John was coaching the swim team, and I was cheering and working full-time, so we didn't have a lot of spare time to spend together. So, John started leaving little notes on my car at school, and I'd leave notes for him. It was a fun relationship at first.

John was my first full-on gay relationship. I've never been the type to have anonymous or casual sex. I was looking for a long-term monogamous relationship from the beginning. John and I met a few times before we finally decided to sleep together. But we always met at The Garage. Although John would go to gay bars, he wasn't fully out. Despite the fact that his parents were psychologists and probably would have been able to handle the news, he had never told them. He was very self-conscious about his sexuality and spent a lot of time trying to maintain a macho persona. This should have been a red flag, but I was too inexperienced in relationships to recognize it.

When I was cheering, John came to the games. At first, I felt like he was very supportive. But then he started to show controlling behavior that kept me from attending some of the extracurricular activities with the squad. He wanted me to attend certain things and do certain things with him; it was always about what John wanted to do. I had gotten myself trapped by thinking that kind of relationship was all I deserved.

His being closeted was very familiar to me, although it was probably not the best environment for my first relationship. On weekends when I wasn't at a game, John would host parties. He was very social and had a lot of friends, albeit highly dysfunctional friends! There would be drugs and alcohol at his parties and, of course, other men. And if John found me talking to any of those men, he would get very jealous. Meanwhile, he would be flirtatious and clingy with some of his friends, whom he swore he was not sexually involved with, but I always had the feeling that he was. I wanted so badly just to be with someone—to be seen and not be alone— that for a long time, I overlooked his jealous streak and other manipulative behaviors. I was malleable, willing to bend in any direction to be more of what he needed.

He, however, did not want to be seen with me. I think he liked the fact that I was a cheerleader, but he wouldn't go out publicly with me. He'd go to some of my games, but he would bring another friend along. I was a bit more open and out than what made him comfortable, so he would be very stoic when next to me outside the house. We never even sat next to each other. It was frustrating, because I held the vision in my head and my heart of being married, with a house and kids...the things everyone else in the world and in the movies seemed to want. I was tired of hiding.

While I was dating John, I came out to my parents. I had grown close to my stepmom, Debbie, by then. To save money during college, I moved in with her and my dad for a while, living in their basement. They lived close to my job at Farmers Insurance, and I figured it was a way to get to know my dad a bit better. My stepmom and I would hang out at the house after my classes, while Dad was working and my two younger half brothers were in school. Since I worked the night shift, I had time to kill, so we'd sit and watch horror flicks or soap operas together—we both loved *The Young and the Restless*. We were watching TV, eating chocolate chip cookies we had just made, when I seized on a moment of courage.

"Debbie, I'd like to share something with you," I paused. "I'm seeing someone. His name is John." I told her about him and how we met; I told her about my theater friends at school and how they introduced me to The Garage and gay bars. She proceeded to tell me a bit about some of the gay friends she'd had in college, and how she was totally fine with it. It was really a fun, nice conversation.

"Now that you know, I'd like to share this with Dad. What do you think?" I wanted to get a pulse on how she thought he'd handle the news.

She was very loving. "I think that's great! You can share this with your dad; he'll be fine," she assured me.

"When do you think I should tell him?" I asked.

She was really helpful in picking out a day when she could intentionally take the boys somewhere so that Dad and I could be alone at the house. I knew there would be no backing out of it that way—we had made a plan, and I had to stick to it. The day came, she left with the boys, and Dad and I were sitting together on the couch.

"I have something I want to tell you," I started nervously. "I've met someone, and I really like them, and I'm really excited about that."

Dad jumped right in. "Well, I know it's hard sometimes when you're dating. Girls can be really challenging."

I swallowed. "Well, Dad, the person I'm dating, his name is John."

Dad stood up, walked over to me, and said, "Stand up—give me a hug." It was just so beautiful. He hugged me and cried and said, "I can't believe you would want to tell me. I'm so proud of you." It was surprising to me how he responded, because I wasn't really close to him since we had lived apart for so long. Coming out to my dad brought us closer together.

It felt really good to know that he knew, and like he was finally giving me permission. He said, "Well, I don't understand. But it's okay. I'm glad you trust me to tell me who you are." I'll never forget that.

My dad had a very troubled childhood himself. He lived with his grandparents after my aunt was born, when he was eight years old. Dad is a very distant person; he has spurts of closeness and then yanks back. So, to have that moment with him was so meaningful. While I wasn't expecting him to yell or respond badly—he's very docile, quiet, and humble—neither was I expecting such quick acceptance and affection. Finally, I felt seen by him. I felt his love in a way I never had before. I had never had a hug like that from him ever; it was always a pat. I had even felt jealousy and insecurity because he was raising two other sons who lived with him and knew him; I'd spent years wondering where I fit in. Now, in that moment, all of that went away. It was just him and me, sharing some time together.

After that, I felt like I could walk into his house, be myself, and talk about John. But the juxtaposition was that my mom didn't handle the news as well as I thought she would. My two coming-outs were completely opposite experiences. I had thought Dad would be the one with the problem and was nervous about telling him; with Mom, I didn't approach it with any trepidation or fear. I approached her casually one day and said, "Hey, I just want you to know I'm dating John." I was surprised when she acted like she didn't know.

"I don't want to hear this," she said, shutting down. "I don't want to know what's going on." I interpreted that as meaning *You can be yourself to a point, but then I don't want to know.*

I thought, *I've been gay since I was five. I know you knew.* I was so disappointed. I was still seeking parental permission and approval; I hadn't yet figured out that I didn't need it.

I never had a full "coming-out" conversation with Granny. I don't think I needed to. She knew who

I was, well before I did. I know she and Grandpa talked about it with each other, and I do remember telling her I had a boyfriend while sitting on the couch, but it just felt like natural conversation. "That's great! I'm very happy for you!" she said. I never felt uncomfortable with her; she always just went with the flow.

By the time John and I graduated in June of '91, we were in our mid-twenties. He wanted to get a PhD in kinesiology and needed to move to Tallahassee to attend Florida State University. So, I left Farmers Insurance and moved to Tallahassee with him. My mom wasn't accepting of the move. I don't know where her hesitancy was coming from—maybe it's because she didn't like John—but nevertheless, she and Grandpa rented a big U-Haul and moved us into our new, beautiful apartment.

John got a job as the swim coach at Florida State University, which contributed to his fears around coming out. He probably would have lost his job if he came out; Tallahassee wasn't as liberal and safe as Columbus, so he was even more terrified of being outed. We still went to gay bars, but he would cover up his license plates with duct tape when he drove there. After we left, we'd pull over at a 7-Eleven, and he'd take the tape off for the remainder of the drive home.

Meanwhile, I kept myself busy working multiple jobs while John was busy with school and not around very much. I got a job as an assistant cheer coach at Florida State. John had told me where the cheer team practiced, and I showed up one day and said to the coach, who was male and a former FSU cheerleader, "If you ever need anything, I'd love to help."

"Oh my gosh, that would be great!" he said.

I was thrilled; I had been missing that part of my life. I also got a job working part-time at Cellular One, selling cell phones, and a job teaching step aerobics at a gym down the street from our apartment.

John and I started growing apart during that time. I was meeting people and making new friends. I started to get tired of John not being open about where he'd be; he'd sneak off somewhere, and I suspected he was sleeping with other people. He never really told anybody that we were a couple, which was very hard for me. Being out in Columbus, I had become more comfortable with myself, and the move to Tallahassee felt like a step backward. Once again, I was not being seen.

For a long time, I bent over backward to do whatever John wanted; I was the people pleaser. But I became increasingly tired of his behavior. We were at a nightclub once, in the middle of nowhere, when he left to go to the restroom. He came back and saw me talking to someone who had approached me. I appreciated how this man was more out and not uptight, which sparked a feeling that not all men were like John. John got jealous and irate; he grabbed me by the arm and said, "We're leaving!"

"I'm not leaving. I don't want to leave." I stood my ground. I stayed, and he left.

John had driven, so I had to find my own way home. After three and a half years, I had finally had enough. We turned the second bedroom in our apartment, which we'd used as an office, into my bedroom and became uncomfortable roommates for a couple of months, until I found another living situation and moved out. I stayed in Tallahassee for six more months, but it didn't feel like home. I missed Columbus.

CHAPTER 8:

Changing Course

"We have a friend who lives in Paris. His name is Doug. He's a dancer at the Moulin Rouge."

I was talking to some cheerleading alumni friends about a year after my breakup with John. I had moved back to Columbus, Ohio, trying to run away from the pain of the failed relationship, despite how dysfunctional it had been. I rented a small apartment with a roommate and waited tables at Dalt's, which is a TGI Fridays chain restaurant. I was depressed and frustrated that my life wasn't taking off. I needed a reset.

I mentioned to my friends that I'd love to go overseas to Europe. Doug was a former Ohio State cheerleader, whom I had never met since he was a few years older than me. "You should reach out to him," my friend insisted.

I was intrigued, so I reached out. Doug welcomed me with enthusiasm. "Sure, come visit! I have plenty of space here, and an extra bed. You can stay with me as long as you'd like."

I saved up some money, got a passport, and flew to Paris, with no real plan for what I'd do or how long I'd stay. From the airport, I took a cab to Doug's apartment and hit the buzzer. He let me in, and I was immediately struck by how handsome he was, to the point that he made me nervous. But I was still hurting from how messed up my last relationship had been, and I had no intention of pursuing a new relationship while in Paris. Besides, Doug was a good guy, and despite everything they put me through, I was still more attracted to bad guys.

Doug introduced me to all his friends. When he was at work, I'd walk around the city sightseeing. Then I'd come back to the apartment, sleep for a bit, and meet up with Doug and his friends at 3:00 a.m. at a café across the street from the Moulin Rouge, where they'd decompress from that night's show. Some nights, we went out clubbing. It was freeing to be in a big city and not feel any pressure to be something I wasn't. Largely because of where we lived and where Doug worked, I was surrounded by gay people; it felt so different from Ohio.

Through Doug, I even auditioned for commercial work while in Paris; it was fun, but none of it led anywhere. After about nine weeks, I was running out of money and had to use the last of it to buy a ticket home. But the trip had served its purpose—it was a nice break from my life and from Ohio, and a perfect reset for me after the breakup.

When I returned to Columbus, I realized I had outgrown it. It had become too small. Since Dalt's was a chain, I could transfer to another restaurant in another state. So, six months after Paris, in 1994, I decided to move to Fort Lauderdale, Florida. I was sitting in my car, all packed up, and my mom was there crying, "Please don't leave, please, please, please." She was so worried about me, which gave me mixed messages. She was normally so stoic. I wasn't raised in a family that shared a lot of emotions; we never talked about feelings. Now, she was showing an outburst of emotion, and I didn't know what to do with it.

I internally handled the situation much like she had handled the conversation when I came out. *I don't know why you're doing this. I don't know how to process this right now. This is weird to me. I've made my decision. I'm leaving.* I said, "I have to go, Mom." I had already made plans and wanted to get the hell out of Columbus, and that was what I was going to do. I didn't see my place there anymore. I felt like I had checked all the boxes and there were bigger and better things out there for me. The Fort Lauderdale–Miami area had a large gay scene, and I had a theater degree and still wanted to pursue acting. I had done some modeling and stage acting with some success in Columbus. Now, I was ready to prove to the world that I was more than just a model. I was ready to live in a place where I could be seen.

Next thing you know, I'm homeless.

I had moved to Florida with someone who said I could stay at his place until I found my own. But within a week, he told me he was moving and I had to get out right away. I had only a few days' notice, and I was freaking out. *Where was I going to go?* I was essentially living in my car.

I looked at the 'roommate wanted' ads in the local gay newspaper and interviewed a homeowner who hired me to take care of his house and cat-sit in exchange for room and board. He travelled a lot for his work, and I lived with him for several years.

Shortly after getting settled in with my new living arrangement in Miami, I started working as a model again. It was still in my head that I was better as a model than an actor. I was having a grand time, though, doing Spanish-speaking commercials and swimsuit photos, and trying to find my niche in the performance world. Even though I didn't speak Spanish, they taught me the lines. *Muy Guapo.* But most of it non-speaking model work. I also was an extra in some films. That's when I met one of my best friends, Bruce, who is a makeup artist. We were standing in line as extras, wearing pool-boy outfits, for *The Specialist* with Sly Stallone and Sharon Stone. While waiting a couple of hours for our scene, we got to talking and hit it off. I felt really comfortable with him; he was a great ball of energy, always laughing and up for an adventure. He's gay, but there wasn't sexual energy between us. It is the one of the strongest male relationships that I have, to this day.

Bruce lived in Miami Beach, which is where all the auditions were held. I would spend the night over at Bruce's sometimes, and we'd go out to clubs and gay bars. I became his sidekick. At that time in my life, that is what I needed: to hang out with a male without any sexual pressure.

I was having fun, but I was struggling financially. I was renting a garage apartment, living as a starving artist while also working at a bank, waiting tables, and selling gym memberships for Club Body Tech. But I had hopes and dreams for more. Becoming an actor was still on my mind; I was still seeking to claim my place in the world. I wanted to act in soap operas. I did some TV commercial work, but the feedback my agent gave me was that I was too feminine, or that my voice wasn't right for the part. I didn't even know what that meant. *Is it because I have a "gay voice"? The inflection or something?* I wondered. *What opportunities have I missed out on because of who I am?* The narrative that I was not good enough, that I should just be a model, played in my head constantly because I wasn't even getting nonspeaking acting parts. I thought maybe I should go into fitness; if I could have a fabulous body and look butch, maybe I could overcome this block.

My job at Club Body Tech led me to spend time with the wrong crowd. One of the trainers at the club was a dance booker; he was responsible for booking all the dancers in all the hottest clubs in Miami and Key West. Because I worked out a lot, he suggested I become a dancer. I was tempted by how lucrative it was. I needed the cash, so I agreed to do it. I mostly danced in Miami Beach and Fort Lauderdale. There was a bar called the Copa in Fort Lauderdale that has since closed down, and another bar called Twist. I would dance wherever I could get a gig at night, and sell memberships during the day.

I wasn't a traditional dancer; I wasn't going to wear a thong—which we called G-strings—like the Chippendales dancers (that was hot at the time). Instead, I wore white briefs, black construction boots, and a ball cap. I had long bangs (model hair!) and would keep the hair over my eyes while wearing the ball cap...I knew how to keep it mysterious. I approached the role as a character I was playing; I had thought it all out...his name was Luke. That was the only way I could get up on that stage. I made a lot of money; I was a rule breaker with my outfit, which became very popular once the other guys saw how much I was making.

Of course, there was a dark side to the business. In the 1970s and '80s, when gay life was not as mainstream as it is today, the gay community had to find ways to meet others like them. We weren't able to be ourselves, and I believe that pushed so many into bad habits of drinking, drugs, and poor sexual decisions. The AIDS crisis was a smack in the face, the "gay cancer" really demonstrated how scarring the world can be when individuals don't have permission to be themselves and have authentic relationships. That feeling of not being able to be fully seen, fully myself, lasted for years. I'm better now, but the internal voice that says, "You aren't worthy," rears its ugly head from time to time. I've learned how to not listen to it, but I think the haunting from that invisibility never fully goes away.

All too often during that time in Miami Beach, we'd get together with friends and everything would be about overindulging in cocktails or drugs, leading up to vomiting in the street after a lovely dinner. I had experimented with alcohol, I had been drunk and gotten sick, but thankfully my desire for more out of life overrode the high from alcohol and drugs. Therefore, during this time, I didn't drink or do drugs and was always the group's designated driver.

Once a month for a year on a Friday or Saturday night, we would dance at a bar in Key West. I drove my black Jeep Cherokee soft top the three hours from Miami Beach to Key West, with the top down and the radio blaring. We would leave at around four o'clock in the afternoon for a 7:00 p.m. arrival. Our first dance set was around 8:00 or 9:00 p.m. We would rotate who was dancing, because it was a smaller bar. Our job was just to dance on the bar; I wore my tighty-whities and got into my dance character. We would step over drinks, and the guys would tip us when we'd get down closer. Each set lasted about fifteen or twenty minutes, and then we would step down and walk the crowd for more tips or just go in the back and wait until it was our turn again. There was never any kind of a choreographed or group Chippendales set; it was one-on-one and mostly out in the open. There were private rooms for guys who were doing a lot more for more money, but I wasn't interested in that. We'd get paid around seventy-five dollars for the dance, plus tips. In 1995, minimum wage was $3.05 an hour, so this was some real money.

We made so much money dancing at that bar that there were some intense opportunities. People were really aggressive in Key West. The patrons felt entitled; they tipped generously, but then they felt like they owned us. There were several times when we had to fight them off because there were hotel rooms above the bar that they were always trying to get us to. Some of the dancers would decide to go up there, and the rest of us would leave. I don't know how they got home. I would drive all the way back at two or three o'clock in the morning down that two-way street, with everyone else passed out in the back seat. We couldn't afford to spend the night in Key West because we would have spent all the money that we just made to stay in a hotel.

I witnessed a lot, but I stayed out of it. Sometimes it was hard not to get sucked into that world, especially since I still wanted so badly to be seen and adored. I wanted to match the level of adoration from a crowd that I had felt at my first solo choir performance, and as a cheerleader at Ohio State. Dancing was somewhat of a commodity for me, as I still felt that what I had with the most value was my sexuality. I believe that is how I saw myself after the incident all those years back in high school with Mr. Collins. Especially once I came out to myself,

I believed I was only worth something to someone because of my sexuality, not my personality.

***

One day at the bank, a client came in and said, "Every time I come to you, your customer service is great. You follow up. We have an event-planning position open that we'd love to talk to you about."

"Well, I don't know," I said. The offer came out of left field. "I'm getting some acting roles, doing commercial work, and making some money," I told her. I didn't mention the dancing work that I did.

"That's okay. You can continue to do that, but let's talk. My name is Michelle."

We went to lunch, and she told me that she was head of a foundation that the Florida-Caribbean Cruise Association (F-CCA) had set up. The foundation's mission was to positively promote the cruise industry in the Caribbean islands; the people of the islands didn't want ships stopping there because they'd dump all their trash. So, the industry had to reestablish dialogue with the island governments and come up with plans to make cruising a win-win for both the cruise industry and the locals.

"I know you have a degree in theater and you're a performer. And that's great." She continued, "Did you realize that events are just like theater?"

I did not. For me, an "event" was a family reunion where everyone went to Granny's house and bought Tupperware. I'd never been to a fundraiser. In rural

Ohio, potlucks or the county fair were "events," but I didn't see them as such. She explained more about the role, we talked it through, and I decided to take the job. That was the job that got me out of dancing and the lifestyle that went along with it, which I had grown tired of.

I became the manager of marketing and events for the FCCA. I started producing events and allowing myself to explore. My job was to fly down to the Caribbean, meet the ship, and organize beach cleanups for the ship staff. Or, we would do things like fly doctors from Miami to perform free medical exams for residents on the island. Then I organized a conference where we sold booths to local island business owners—makers of rum, cakes, jewelry, art, and so forth—for them to promote their products. Cruise executives would attend the conference, sample products, and purchase orders for the ships to sell to passengers. The events were economic drivers for the islands. I also planned an annual gala in Fort Lauderdale to raise money for the work that the foundation did. I saw firsthand how much an organization can raise to provide services directly; it was a great fit for me, combining work that I was passionate about with work that served communities.

Because Michelle had planted the seed that events are like theater, I took everything I learned from theater and applied it to my job. This would turn out to be a pivotal distinction of my approach, and I use it as a guiding principle for events to this day. I ensured that we had the lights coordinated with the decor, and the decor coordinated with the entertainment, and the entertainment coordinated with the food. I hit all the senses, making the event theatrical and interesting, rather than just ho-hum rubber chicken with someone talking for forty-five minutes at a podium.

Getting my degree in theater had been beneficial because it expanded my horizons. I'd had to take classes like scene shop, costuming, and theater history, as well as subjects on the technical side of theater. To earn my BA, I had to be a stage manager, which is basically an event planner. Stage managing is creating and completing a checklist of everything that needs to happen, including rehearsals and coordinating with the director, costume designer, scene designer, and lighting designer. All of that went into event planning. Event planning is a full expression of my theater background. It incorporates all my creativity and flare. The HR professional at Farmers Insurance had said, "Go get a degree in something you love." I chose theater. That job got me started in event planning, which I still work in today. But I wasn't yet ready to give up my acting dream.

***

I lived in Fort Lauderdale for four years, until December 1998, when I decided to move to Los Angeles. I had friends who lived there, and I thought I would give it a shot and see whether I could make it on the big screen! I drove my four-door Honda Civic across the country with all my worldly possessions. Everything I owned fit in that car. I got my Screen Actors Guild (SAG) card and got an agent at age twenty-seven, which is unheard of. I was determined to be an actor, but all the while I held in my heart that I wanted a family—a husband, kids, and a house.

I had a friend from the theater department at Ohio State who was now living in Los Angeles with her husband, and they graciously allowed me to sleep on their couch until I could find a job. I stayed there for three weeks until I landed the front desk night shift at Gold's Gym in Hollywood, waiting for my big break. I'd show up in the late afternoon and work until the gym closed at midnight. I checked people in, told visitors about our memberships, and then turned them over to a salesperson. I made enough there to rent a small studio apartment at Hollywood and Vine. It was a very downtrodden neighborhood at the time; today, the area has been revitalized.

The gym was in the gay mecca of Hollywood; every night, I dealt with propositions and people hitting on me. Some of the guys were relentless. Many of them were older men, working on beautiful bodies, waiting for the same big break that I was. They would tell me about their auditions and how they'd failed to get the part. I had been going to auditions as well, and although I hadn't gotten a part yet, people told me I was doing great for being there such a short time. But seeing these people at the gym started painting a picture of what my future could look like. *I don't want to be seventy years old and still hoping for my big break*, I thought.

By the end of the night, it was often just me left alone to lock up. I was responsible for the cash drawer, so it wasn't really safe. When I left, there was always something going on outside—cops arresting someone up the street or a homeless person asking me for money. Sometimes when I was locking up, I had to step over drunk and drugged-out people lying on the steps of the gym. One night, I stepped out the door to find a drunken, drugged-out drag queen, with makeup smeared all over their face and their wig strewn on the pavement.

"Um, I have to lock up. You have to move..."

No response, of course.

As I was bending down, trying to move them so I could lock the door, it hit me like a ton of bricks: *What the hell am I doing here?!* I thought. *What the hell would my mom think if she saw this?!* I never did tell her. *I'm so much better than this.* It was the last straw. I had been in Los Angeles only nine months, but I'd had enough. I felt alone, certain that this was not the life I'd envisioned for myself. I was impatient and wanted things to happen fast. I was twenty-seven years old already, and I felt I was running out of time for an acting career. In that moment, I accepted that being an actor wasn't going to happen for me.

Three days later, Grandma Kingham died of lung cancer. I had just returned from a trip home, during which I had visited her in the hospital. At the time, no one thought she was dying; she was sick, and they were trying to find a diagnosis, but everyone thought she was going to be okay. We had no idea yet that it was cancer. I'd flown back to LA, only to return to work and have to step over passed-out drag queens. When I got the news that she'd died, I knew what I had to do. *I wasn't with my grandma when she died*, I thought with sadness. *I am missing important things at home...for this?!* I put in my notice at work and called Granny.

"I want to move back to Columbus," I told her, "but I need help." I started crying. I was so embarrassed by what I was about to say.

"Go ahead, Tracy—you can ask me anything."

"I'm broke. I can barely make my rent and car payment. Can you loan me some money?" I knew she had the money, but it killed me to have to ask her for it; I was a grown adult, yet here I was running to my grandma for my most basic expenses. She lent me $2,500 so I could buy myself out of my lease and pay for gas and hotel rooms on the drive home. I left really early in the morning; I remember looking back in the rearview mirror, listening to Madonna sing "Ray of Light," and saying goodbye to that dream.

Looking back, I think I could have made the dream come true with more time and the right mindset. I had an excellent acting coach who was taking my skills to places they had never been. I was really just getting started. But I had so much destructive mind chatter from high school and college—I wasn't good enough, I was too effeminate, I should stick with modeling—that all I knew how to do was hide. I wasn't fully comfortable with who I was yet, and that came through in my acting. But acting itself meant pretending to be somebody else—when I just wanted to be me! Looking back at gay characters in film and TV from the '90s, I see they were all pretty stereotypical; I think there would have been a place for me if I had stuck it out, but I would have had to compromise myself. Gay characters were usually the butt of the joke, and that would have hurt.

I moved back home and got a job with Big Brothers Big Sisters, and began slowly working to rebuild my life and pay Granny back.

CHAPTER 9:

The House, the Kids, the Wedding

My personal life was in a bit more turmoil than my professional life. Dating controlling men was a pattern for me. I started seeing another man named Carlos, who had a lot of the same coping mechanisms as John—drinking and partying and seeking stimulation outside the relationship, with other gay men at bars. The bar scene didn't feel like me. As I had with John, I was morphing to fit in and make Carlos happy so I could keep the relationship alive. I kept trapping myself by thinking, *They're so into me—this is great!* and allowing the physical stuff to drive the relationship, rather than an emotional or a mental connection.

I pursued that relationship heavily, and we ended up living together. Carlos had warned me that he was a player and not "relationship material," but mistakenly, I thought I could turn him around. Of course, now I know that people don't change unless they choose to change for themselves. I'm not even sure what that relationship was all about for me, other than going after what I thought I wanted—and maybe what I was told, by Carlos, that I couldn't really have. Once again, somebody in my life was telling me I couldn't go after what I wanted. After a couple of years, I accepted that I couldn't change him and that he was not what I wanted anyway.

At the time, gay bars were where gay men had to go to be around like-minded individuals. They were the playground, if you will, for being gay. There was nowhere else to go, aside from house parties. Gay culture had to be behind closed doors, since it was not safe to be ourselves in public. However, without permission to fully be ourselves, many headed down a path of destruction, which sometimes put us in dangerous situations. Many times, I'd leave a club and there'd be characters at the back door, wanting something from me that I didn't want to give.

One guy I dated carried a butcher knife in his coat pocket and kept knives under his bed. He didn't trust the world. That freaked me out; I found it creepy and weird. When I broke up with him, I took him out to dinner intentionally so we would be in a public place. He took out the knife and plunged it into the table. *Okay, I've had enough of the bad boys*, I finally decided. I knew it was time to deal with the dysfunction in my relationship patterns.

Believe it or not, I first got into therapy for business reasons. I had left California by then, worked as an events manager for Big Brothers Big Sisters for a year and a half, and then started working with a company called Limited Brands as their events manager. I really loved the job; it pushed me to levels of excellence I never thought I could reach. I was truly being seen and adored, and that felt great. There was, however, a lot of pressure to perform at that level in a corporate job. While there, I learned what it meant to be an entrepreneur—to push the boundaries to create an experience. I started thinking that I had what it took to go out on my own, and I realized I could probably make better money and have more creative freedom running my own show. I had worked at Limited Brands for over four years and was ready for a new kind of challenge.

Looking back, watching my mom and Granny run their own businesses was the perfect training ground for entrepreneurship. From a young age, I worked alongside my mom, cutting out her artwork, carving the frames and staining them, packaging them, and selling them to stores. Then there was helping her and Granny in their ceramics studios. Creative and business spirits were always within me. However, to help me make the decision to go out on my own, I hired a business coach named Suzanne, who was more like a therapist. She explained that a personal life and a business life are kind of the same; you can't just come into an office and turn off your personal life.

She suggested, "Why don't you try something different with your dating relationships?" She encouraged me not to sexualize the relationship from the beginning. "Look at compatibility first. What type of a person are they?" This approach was really a challenge for me, because I didn't really know who I was.

With dating, I constantly felt unworthy, not good enough. So I was always attracted to the bad boys, or the guys who treated me poorly right from the beginning. I didn't think I was good enough to have what I really wanted, which was a husband, my own business, the house with the lawn and the kids playing in the back—the dream that many people have. I felt that was the next stage in life for me, but it was something that I thought I couldn't have, because I was who I was. All the noise from growing up had me thinking that gay people didn't deserve to have fulfilling lives.

Suzanne walked me through how to approach relationships differently. She told me to get to know a man first, ask a lot of questions, and see if there was compatibility. "Also ask yourself if this person will be supportive of your business. Because running a business is going to take a lot of your time," she wisely suggested.

***

When I broke up with Butcher Knife Guy, I had my own small house in Columbus. I was in my back bedroom with my giant, clunky computer, which took up most of the desk, working away, when my friends called me.

"Hey Trace, we're having a Fourth of July party. Want to come?"

I thought it sounded like fun, so I went. There was a wide variety of people there. I saw my friends Scott and John, who had introduced me to Butcher Knife Guy. They came over and said, "I know it didn't work out with what's-his-name, but our friend Brad just moved to Columbus. You guys would really hit it off."

"No thanks," I said. *I am not doing this whole setup thing again*, I thought.

"Oh, come on, you've got to meet this guy. He's really great." I don't know why they were so worried about me dating someone, but I guess they were just trying to be nice.

I kept insisting, "No, thanks, I'm good." I had just started my business earlier that year and was content focusing on my career.

Fast-forward to Halloween of that year. I went to the same house, which was in a small farming community. The homeowner was a producer for *Country Living* magazine, and we were there for a photo shoot; we all wanted the opportunity to be in a magazine. The party was fabulous. Scott and John approached me again. "You know, Brad just bought a house down the street from where you live. You live on Hanford, right?"

"Yeah, I live on Hanford Street."

"Well, he's up by High Street, 19 Hanford."

"Oh, okay, great." I still didn't think much of it.

"You guys should meet. He's such a great guy. We think you'd hit it off."

"No thanks, not interested."

Fast-forward to December. I went to a drag show with another set of friends and there were Scott and John.

"Hey, how are you guys doing?" I went over to say hello.

"Hi, Trace. This is Brad." Brad turned around, and I was instantly enamored. Six-foot-four, tall, beefy, broad-shouldered, obscenely handsome. *Brad.* We locked eyes, and it was magic. We talked, very uncomfortably and for a short time, because I was nervous. I gave him my business card and said, "Let's get together some time."

"Yeah, that'd be great," he replied. I turned around, and he smacked me on the ass.

After he left, I told my friend Darryl, "I'm going to spend the rest of my life with that guy."

"You're crazy. Let's go get a beer." That's Darryl.

So, of course I told my therapist that I met Brad. She wasn't as enthused as I was. "Slow down," she warned. "The attraction is there, and that's good, but you don't have to act upon that now. This is the opportunity to get to know him. Find out if he's compatible, not just another disappointment in your life."

We'd worked through all these different questions in therapy. I don't remember writing them down, but I had them ready in my mind. Adoption was one of them. I wanted to find someone who wanted to adopt children. That was my vision of what I wanted for my life—after starting my own business and buying a BMW. After I started my business, Suzanne told me to go and buy the BMW, even though I really couldn't afford it. "When you want something and you go after it, you find a way to make it work," she said. And I did—I got another business contract and was able to pay for that BMW. Now for the husband.

On Christmas Eve, I was driving home and turned onto my street. Well, Brad's house was right there, and he was backing into his garage. I came around in my car—not my BMW, which was in the garage— but my little Honda Civic. "Oh, shit" flashed through my mind, because I wanted to impress him. *I should be in my Beamer.* I went around the alley and pulled in. Brad was walking out of his detached garage at the back of his house. I came through the alley, swerved around, stopped, rolled down the passenger window, and yelled, "Hey, is that the sexy stud that lives here?"

Who the hell is this? I could see written on his face. Then he got closer and realized it was me. I could see his discomfort, because it had been three weeks since the party and I had not heard from him.

"Why didn't you call?" I asked.

"Well, I didn't realize...I just..." he stumbled to find words to explain. He later told me he hadn't called because he was so into me that he was nervous about getting turned down.

"I'm not a slut," I teased him. "I don't give my business card to everybody."

He laughed and said, "What are you doing for Christmas?"

"I just got home from Target. I'm getting ready to go to my dad's tonight." He told me he was going to his family's later that day.

"Well, call me," I replied. "You've got my number. Have a wonderful Christmas." I still didn't have his number.

Well, he didn't call before I went to LA for New Year's Eve.

Of course, he called me while I was in LA, wanting to get together for the Ohio State football game at AMC Theatre on New Year's Day with Scott and John. He thought that a group setting would be easier on his nerves than going out just the two of us.

"No, I'm in Los Angeles," I said. But I had been thinking about him constantly. "Give me your number, and I'll call you when I get back." So, I got his number.

There was a big snow storm a couple days after my return, and the city basically shut down, so I figured it was a good time to call.

"Hey, what are you doing? Are you working today?" I asked.

"No, I'm just sitting around watching the news."

"Okay, well let's get together sometime," I said. He agreed, and we hung up. Then I heard Suzanne in my head: "Do something different. Do something different." I called him back and said, "Well, you just said you're not doing anything. I'm not doing anything now, either. I mean, I'm here. Do you want to come over?"

"Umm...okay." I think he thought he was coming over for a little nookie but I had a completely different plan in place. I really took my therapist's advice to heart. He sat on one end of the couch. I sat on the other end of the couch. While I was waiting for him to arrive, I took out my little notebook and jotted down my list of questions.

"Let's talk about Brad," I said. I wanted to see if he was compatible. I asked him questions about his likes and dislikes, and what he was looking for in a relationship. The biggest question was: "What do you think about kids? I want to start a family—how do you feel about that?" I wanted to get as much information as I could. I was in my mid-thirties; it was time to get this show on the road. I was checking in to make sure the relationship went beyond a strong physical attraction. For each question, I gave my response as well. It was a two-way street.

"I'm open to that. I actually looked into adoption when I lived in New York. I explored taking a class," he answered.

Okay, check, I thought. That was the big check, because this was the early 2000s. There were not a lot of adoptions happening for gay men. Gay marriage wasn't recognized. It was a very different time. And while adoption was doable, we would have to get creative legally to make it happen. It was a quagmire that we knew we would have to work through.

We spent about two hours sitting on the couch, me drilling him with questions. The attraction was there, and it was all I could do not to jump on him. But I had Suzanne in my head, saying, "Do something different." Eventually, he got up, we hugged, and I said, "Thanks for coming over." I kicked his ass out. I'm sure he was like, "Okay, that was the weirdest thing ever."

We made plans to meet for dinner a couple days later. It was the most awkward dinner...it was completely silent. We went to Cap City, a popular place in Columbus. We were sitting at a little two-top table, struggling with what to talk about. I had already exhausted all the questions I had. I left there not really sure that he was into me. At therapy, I explained what had happened.

"Well, if you feel like it's a good fit, see how it plays out," she suggested.

We went out again and had a good time. We started to relax. I gave him a kiss on the cheek before I got out of the car. This went on for a couple of months. Then one night, we went to a popular restaurant in the German Village, followed by a dance performance. We were sitting in the theater during intermission when I abruptly said, "We need to leave."

"Why?" he asked.

I had eaten a chicken spinach wrap at the restaurant, and it clearly was not sitting well with my stomach. "I'm not feeling well. We really need to leave." We got in his car. "I need you to drive fast,"

I instructed him. I was otherwise going to go to the bathroom in my pants, and I knew how much pride he took in his vehicle. That would be the end of our relationship, for sure. I was mortified by the whole situation; we hadn't even been intimate yet. "Can you just go in the back, through the alley?" I asked. There was a bathroom by the back door of my house. "Just drop me off."

I didn't even say goodbye. I went through the gate, ran to the house, and put the key in the door—and everything let loose in my pants right there. I had to throw everything out: my shoes, my socks, my belt, my pants, my shirt. To this day, I have never eaten another chicken spinach wrap.

Our relationship was saved. And as hard as it was, I continued to do things differently and not give in to habits of the past. I'd talk to myself before going out: "Okay, we're going to go out, but we're not going to stay overnight together. I'm going to come home." Of course, Brad had no idea that I was having these conversations with myself, or with a therapist. But despite the relationship not getting physical, he kept coming back for more. Most men would have probably given up.

Fast-forward to not long after Valentine's Day. I invited him over. I made dinner—salad, steak and risotto, and a molten chocolate cake (homemade, of course). I got my friend Angie, who was a massage therapist, to set up a massage table in my bedroom. I lit a hundred-plus candles in the bedroom, unbeknownst to him, of course. I had written a little note to go with each course. With the last course, after dessert, he opened a note that told him to go upstairs. It said, "I've hired a massage therapist. His name is Sven. Sven is going to give you a nice massage. P.S. You can't touch Sven." He went upstairs and got disrobed and under the towel. I changed into a white T-shirt, white jeans, and white socks and shoes. Then I came in and spoke in a different voice. I was Sven.

I started massaging him. He didn't realize I was Sven at first, because I was wearing a different outfit than I'd worn at dinner. But once he realized it was me, all bets were off. It was very romantic, with all the candles. That's when we realized that the relationship was going to work.

Brad and I decided to date officially. Six months later, I moved in with him for a brief period of time, before we decided we needed a bigger home that could accommodate kids. I sold my house, he sold his house, and we bought an old house from 1914 together. It was a four-square, four-bedroom brick home with a front porch, in Grandview Heights, and it needed a lot of work. The plumbing didn't work properly, the electrical wiring was all knob and tube, and the HVAC needed to be replaced. Our cosmetic priorities were getting the bedrooms painted and cleaned up with new hardwood floors. What I loved about the house was that all four bedrooms were on the same floor; we could envision having kids and hearing them across the hallway.

Once the house was renovated, we knew we were ready to bring children into our lives. We got started with the adoption classes and searched for an agency. We belonged to a church community that was very open, located in a gay area of Columbus. Through the church, we met a lesbian couple that had found an agency in Akron that would work with gay couples. The agency shared that they regularly had requests from birth mothers for same-sex couples; before that, we had thought about going international, thinking that we'd have more opportunities to adopt from abroad. Now, we learned that we could adopt domestically. We were asked to compile a little book about our family. We described who we were, what we liked to do, what our home was like, and members of our family. Once all the paperwork was complete, which took about nine months, it was just a matter of weeks before we got our first call. We had been told it might take a year or more! They presented a sibling set to us, but they were not the right fit; they were older children, and we had our hearts set on a baby.

We decided to hold a drumming circle to manifest our shared vision, with the help of a spiritual leader. My dad, my stepmom, and some close friends joined us. Aside from holding our intention in their hearts, they also gave us confidence in our decision. They told us how great we were going to be as parents, and that they were going to support us once we had children. During that time, there was light rain outside. It was May, and we had the window open to let in some air, which meant we could hear what was going on outside. Suddenly, we heard children's laughter. We looked out the window but didn't see anyone. We continued with the drumming circle and considered the laughter to have been a sign.

Five weeks later, on a Saturday night, we got another call from the adoption agency. We were with friends, getting ready to go to a gay men's choir concert. "It's your lucky day," the social worker said. "We have a baby boy available. We need you both to come to the agency tomorrow for an interview." His birth mom named him Nicholas. When we later did the math, we learned that his mother had gone into labor the day that we had held the drumming circle. She had been washing her car when labor started. She rushed to the hospital and gave birth. For a few weeks, she tried to parent the baby by herself, but it wasn't working for her; she was homeless and already had a three-year-old. Nicholas's birth father had said that he would help but didn't. She contacted the agency, had an interview with them, and placed the child up for adoption on the spot. She was given a portfolio of adoptive families to review, and we were called in for an interview, serendipitously to be held on Father's Day, 2006.

"Don't get discouraged if the mother doesn't choose you as parents," the social worker from the agency told us. "You'll probably have to interview four or five times before you get chosen for a child." Brad and I were the last couple to be interviewed. We were led into a room with the mother and the social worker, where we shared a bit about ourselves and the future we envisioned for her child.

Then, the mother turned to the social worker. "Can I say it?" she asked.

"Let's step out of the room for a moment," the social worker replied.

Brad and I were left alone. "I think we're getting this baby, Brad," I said to him anxiously.

"No, they told us we'd have to interview multiple times before we get a child."

The mother and the social worker returned to the room. "We'd like for you to be the parents," they announced.

We couldn't believe it! We hugged each other tight and cried. We were simultaneously overjoyed, scared, and unprepared. What followed was a whirlwind. The social worker kept Nicholas overnight. We had nothing; she gave us a long list of all the things that we had to have ready and in place before we could actually bring Nicholas home. We spent the night in a hotel in Akron so that we could meet with the agency again the next morning, complete all the necessary paperwork, and drive home with the baby.

The night we spent in a hotel, our friends—the lesbian couple from church—came to our house and put together a bassinet, so we'd at least have a place for the baby to sleep when we got home. We went to Target and filled a shopping cart with all the items on the list we'd been given from the agency—a car seat, formula, bottles, diapers, a Pack 'n Play. The next morning, we were handed the baby. Brad and I looked at him, then at each other.

"What do we do now?" Brad asked.

"I don't know. I don't know what I'm doing either." We laughed. We'd figure it out.

Those first few weeks and months were pure exhaustion. Despite the lessons our friends with children had tried to pass on to us, we initially both stayed up together when the baby cried each night. We finally learned that was unsustainable; I could function on one sleepless night, but not multiple sleepless nights in a row. So, we took turns, one parent on duty each night. Nicholas got sick with rotavirus about two weeks after we brought him home; he was vomiting all night and having diarrhea. I'll never forget that odor. We had to use an eyedropper to get fluids in him, while constantly on the phone with the doctor and accepting all the help we could get from my stepmom. We also had regular visits from the social worker over the first six months, until the adoption process could be completed. She was there to ensure that we were bonding with the baby, and she was available as a resource for anything we needed.

It was a challenging time for my relationship with Brad. We were each trying to bond with this child, who had completely interrupted our lives, while the two of us were physically and emotionally drained. I made matters worse by allowing the voices in my head—saying that I didn't deserve a baby, that I wasn't worthy—to cause me to overcompensate and try to prove that I was a good parent. It didn't help that, when we first walked into our home with Nicholas in our arms, my mother was lying on the couch waiting for us with her first words: "Do you know what you've just done?" I never learned the full intention behind those words, but they were painful to hear. My mom was not very supportive of the adoption. I wanted so badly to prove her wrong, partly because there's this narrative in the media that gay people shouldn't be adopting, that we're not good parents, that we're sexual predators. Those messages were emphasized when we went to finalize Nicholas's adoption in front of a judge in Columbus.

After waiting the legally required six months after placement, we got our court date and went before the judge. The adoption agency had all their records. We were ready to finalize and make it official that Nicholas would forever be our child. I had an event space ready for us to celebrate afterward; we had hired a caterer, and our families were already at the court—Brad's family, my family, and some of our friends. In the courtroom, the adoption agency lawyer came over to us and said, "We have a problem." We were all pressed and gussied, with no indication that there was going to be a challenge; it was just a matter of the judge signing the paperwork, and it was over. But this was a very right-wing judge. The lawyer continued, "The judge has a concern about finalizing this adoption. We need witnesses."

"What?" I said. "Okay, we can get witnesses." We called our pastor, and he came down. My stepmom was already there, as were a couple of family friends who could act as witnesses.

"Why should they be parents?" the judge asked. Under official records, he asked them questions about our sexuality, our "sexual deviance," whether or not we were predators, and why they thought we were fit to be parents. It was really inappropriate, very disturbing, and in front of our families. "What does the baby's mother have to say about them?" he asked.

"She interviewed multiple families, and she chose them," the lawyer answered.

"Did she sign her rights away?" the judge asked.

"Yes, we have all the official paperwork and signatures."

"Well, her opinion doesn't matter." The judge was looking for any excuse he could find to make us look unfit.

Our lawyer turned to us. "This isn't going well. Let's pull it." We pulled the case before he could go any further.

"Why are we pulling this?" the judge smirked.

"Because it doesn't sound like you're going to sign," our lawyer answered.

"I haven't made my rendering," he said.

But we didn't want him to render. We knew the issue was that Nicholas was a blond-haired, blue-eyed boy...why would a gay couple deserve a blond-haired, blue-eyed boy? If he were an African American or Hispanic child, I don't know that the judge would've played this game with us.

The situation represented another instance of being told, "You can't do this." I went hog wild to prove that I was a good parent. We had the option of bringing the case in the county where we lived, which was what we tried first, or we could do it in the county where Nicholas was born, which was Summit County. We moved the case to Summit County.

After that experience, Brad and I put a campaign together to get a Democratic judge in place during the next election. It was the first time I had gotten involved in politics so directly. We held fundraisers at our house and shared our story with anyone who would listen, to help remove that individual, who was not following the law, as a judge. He was replaced in the next term, and we like to think we had something to do with that.

We brought our case to Summit County and had our court date a couple of months after the previous one. This time, it was a beautiful experience. It went completely the way it should have gone the first time. We all took a picture with the judge, then went home as the proud, official parents of Nicholas. Three years later, we decided to go through the whole process again—we wanted to adopt a second child. The second time was much easier. We knew what to expect and were therefore less fearful. This time, the agency connected us to a woman who was pregnant with a baby girl. We had specifically asked for a baby girl, and we were delighted they'd found us a match! There were three months left to go before delivery, so we had time to plan for the baby's arrival. We painted one of the bedrooms pink, hung a crystal chandelier, and bought white furniture.

We communicated with the mother throughout the process, and we had already bonded with her and the baby by the time we went to the hospital during a stress test she needed to have, since they were going to induce her. Suddenly, the technician asked, "Why does all the paperwork say baby girl?"

"Because that's what the doctor told me I was having..." the mother answered, confused.

The technician turned the screen around and pointed to proof that the baby was, indeed, a boy! We all looked at each other, unsure of what to say. We could have backed out at that point; we had asked for a girl, and no one would have faulted us for our decision. Instead, Brad and I looked at each other and said, "Okay. Here we go again!"

We were hosting a political fundraiser and had a house full of strangers when we learned that the birth mother was going to be induced to give birth. We rushed out of our home and to the hospital, leaving our friends to manage the fundraiser. It was 6:30 a.m. the following day, and we were at twenty-four hours without sleep, when the doctor said, "We're going to have to do a C-section if we don't deliver in a couple hours since her water has broken." After that news, I was so tired. I talked to Brad about leaving to go back to the hotel to check on Nicholas and our babysitter, who was also with the birth mother's three-year-old son. Brad said it wouldn't be a good idea to leave. So, I went to the bathroom to splash some water on my face.

While I was gone, the birth mother grabbed Brad's arm and said, "The baby is here!" Brad jumped up to uncover her and instantly, out popped Donavan. Brad literally caught him! After a bit of panic, he laid Donavan down on the bed. Donavan didn't make a noise, then Brad heard a whimper, said, "Thank god!" and called the nurse right away. She was calm on the phone and came down to see what Brad needed. Then she panicked. The nurse was calling everyone.

They sent someone to find me. I heard a little knock on the men's bathroom door, and she asked, "Are you Trace?"

"Yes," I said.

"They need you in the room," she said. I quickly went back toward the room and saw Brad pacing.

"Where were you?" he asked. I was literally gone for five minutes and missed our child's birth! But Brad got to cut the umbilical cord, and I got to give Donavan his first bath. The room began filling with physicians and nurses, and the medical director was there too. Luckily it all turned out okay! Donavan weighed in at four pounds, twelve ounces. He fit in one hand.

It was an amazing experience when we got home that day. We had to quickly get our newborn up to the third floor, where Nicholas and our friend Alison were waiting for us. Nicholas wanted to hold him. It was beautiful—he was so sweet. We have an amazing photo of our boys meeting each other for the first time. It is such a great memory for Brad and me.

This time, the court date for the adoption went smoothly on the first try. We had a small gathering with close family and friends at the house to celebrate finally closing the adoption.

In 2013, Brad and I got married in New York City, where our marriage would be legally recognized. Our ceremony was at a little place called the Russian Tea Room. We were surrounded by twelve close friends and family members. Our boys were both there, dressed in the same cream-colored tuxedos with red accents that Brad and I wore. My mother watched live from a video stream. My stepmom was very supportive. Two years later, on June 26, 2015, we had national recognition of our marriage and changed all our last names to Bowman-Kingham.

CHAPTER 10:

Permission to Be Me

When I think about where the internal strength to overcome one's circumstances comes from, for me it came from inborn defiance. When someone told me there was something that I couldn't do, it made me say, "You are wrong. I can do this." I had always thought of defiance as a negative trait, but now I see it positively. It means questioning the world around us. I was aware from a young age that there were consequences to being defiant in rural Ohio. Yet, I had an attitude that, at all costs, I was going to do what it took to be me. That served me in some ways, but not enough to overcome my desire to seek acceptance from the outside world.

Even after I made the cheerleading team, instead of feeling joyful and celebrated, I remember coming home and sitting alone in the walk-in closet upstairs, crying. I had worked my butt off and deserved to be on the team, but I still felt unworthy. In hindsight, I thought if I could just make the team, I would find acceptance from others. I thought I'd hear, "He's making our school look good. We're proud of him." But that didn't happen for me. I carried that feeling of not being worthy all the way through college, when I tried out for cheerleading again. Even though I made the team, I wondered if I was good enough. I don't recall celebrating my accomplishment or having that rite of passage. I never gave myself permission to celebrate the wins. I carried this attitude with me into my professional life.

After seeing the business coach/therapist who led me to meet Brad, I went out on my own as an event planner. In 2003, I had met a woman named Diane at a networking function who said, "We have an event at the Red Cross that we're doing, and we're looking for a new producer. Would you be interested?" I felt very confident about doing work for a nonprofit; I had a lot of experience in that realm. I submitted a proposal, and it was accepted. The Red Cross became my very first client under my own business, and twenty years later, I'm still working with them today.

I love using my passion for event planning as a way to help people. I've made a conscious decision to work only with nonprofits, because it allows me to help organizations and communities that need to raise financial support to fulfill their mission. I see my Granny represented in that choice; the essence of a nonprofit is delivering resources to people who can't otherwise afford them. Granny was a socialite who loved the world of appearances, but she also took on the responsibility of helping others. She had a platform, and she used it for good. I hope I am making her spirit proud.

My career journey has been full of lessons. When I started out on my own in event planning, I knew I was very good at what I did, but when I produced fabulous events, I always looked at them through a lens of criticism. An event for the James Cancer Hospital in Columbus, Ohio, stands out in my mind. The event raised millions of dollars. I took the theme I'd been given, Pirates of the Caribbean, and went in a completely unique direction with it. The event was held in an athletic facility; it was a steel building with a football field in the center and a track around it. We divided the facility into sections with twenty-foot-high drapes hanging in between them from the ceilings, so the guests couldn't see what was beyond. They entered the cocktail room, which had ice sculptures, music, and a bar. While guests were there, we had actors dressed in pirate costumes climb up into the rafters in the dining room, where they would sit concealed until dessert. When we were ready for the guests to move into the dining room, we blew a foghorn to suggest that the boat was going to leave, lifted the tasseled drape, and led them into the dining room. There was a circular stage on the other end of the room, with one hundred beautifully decorated tables in front. The centerpieces were flowers in vases that had fish swimming inside, lit up from underneath. Behind the stage was the catering section.

During dessert, all the servers wore pirate hats and handed out glow sticks and beads from treasure chests. Some of them came out with swords and started play fighting. Finally, the actors in the rafters came flying down through the air to take over the "ship." The DJ started playing music, and it became a big dance party. It was pretty spectacular—far different from any other event the guests had seen.

The client loved it and sang my praises, until her sister-in-law told her that it was "kind of hokey." Instead of celebrating how much the event had raised and how much the guests had loved it, I clung to the negative—the one person out of 1,200 at the dinner who had called it hokey! That event went on to win several awards; it put me on the map in Columbus. People saw what I could bring creatively to the event-planning scene. But I still didn't celebrate it. It took therapy to help me realize that I have to be the one to initiate celebrating the wins.

Therapy brought that pattern to light, as did talking to some people who are close to me. "Look at all the things that you've accomplished that so many have never done," they said. I've since learned, and am trying to instill in my children, that we all have to start somewhere. Being an entrepreneur is a great learning ground for breaking old patterns. As an entrepreneur, you have to be your own cheerleader. There is no team of people celebrating you. It's just you. You wear the hat of leader and encourager, light a fire under your own ass, show up to work, and get the work done. As you build a team, that changes, but you're still always responsible for generating income for yourself—and all the actions that are required in order to make that happen. Therefore, I had to learn how not to seek encouragement from outside of myself.

I did, however, end up getting that kind of encouragement, too. I had been producing events for the Red Cross for years—I did this event that I was very proud of, for what was called Humanitarian of the Year. We had a huge screen behind the stage that we made look like the front page of the newspaper because *The Columbus Dispatch*, which was owned by a very influential family in Columbus, had been the main sponsor for years. Throughout the program, we changed the photos and headlines to match the story the speaker was talking about. We got to the end, where we were honoring a family. I had a photo of the family on the screen with the headline "Your Red Cross Honors Humanitarian of the Year." I submitted that event to the International Special Events Society, now called the International Live Events Association, and placed as a finalist. Brad and I went to New Orleans, and they called my name to go to the stage. That's when I realized that I really had something, and I was crying because I felt I had never been celebrated. I went up there, and it was all I could do to talk without breaking down. Afterward, I thought, *Why was I such a blub-berer?* It's because I knew what I had done was good, just like I knew my cheerleading was good. I stood up there in disbelief that I was being recognized at an international level for the work that I did. I didn't think I was going to win, even though I knew in my heart that I should.

I was finally feeling seen. It felt like a full circle moment. I thought about my first taste of the stage after my choir solo, and the sweetness of the applause. I thought about how I'd survived Richard Kipman and bullying from all these kids who said, "You're not good enough." I thought of that little boy in high school who was five-foot-six and tiny, walking around looking for validation, wanting to be seen. Now I realize that not being like everybody else is what set me apart. That wasn't a weakness; it was my power. That's when I started to tell myself, *You have permission to be you.*

Ironically, that realization led me to realize that I wasn't giving my own kids—or my husband, for that matter—full permission to be themselves.

***

As our kids grew up, I started to understand the role of a parent with regard to permission. I had always sought permission from the adults in my life. My therapist once asked, "What were you hoping for as a child?"

I said, "Permission to be me." But now that I am an adult with kids myself, I understand that parents' role is to teach kids to give themselves permission.

My journey has been one of learning that I don't need my parents' permission, the community's permission, or the government's permission to be myself—to be with the person I love, to have children as a gay man, to get married. It's a parent's role to help their child learn independence and self-governance. But where is that transition? I certainly would have benefited if the adults in my life had given me permission early on to be myself, and then handed that responsibility off to me as I grew up, i.e., "We love you just as you are, and now it is up to you to go into the world and be yourself."

Since being told there was something I couldn't do made me want to prove that I could do it, I decided early on that I was going to be the best parent. *Yeah, right.* Striving to be the best in this respect had a negative impact on my relationships. I could have just focused on the fact that we'd made our dream come true—that because of our coming together, we were able to be parents! But I was still learning. In some ways, I shut Brad out when it came to parenting. It was often my way or the highway—how we would feed them, how we would dress them, how we would nurture them. I had this fear that if we didn't present as perfect parents—whatever I thought that looked like in the moment—then someone would swoop in and take our children away, because we were gay. I also feared we didn't deserve them.

I'm sure I hurt Brad many, many times by insisting that my way was the better way to parent, rather than approaching things from the perspective of how we could parent together as a couple. Brad is and always has been a great parent, but I sought control anyway. I thought that if I was in control, I could ensure that the outcome would be what I needed it to be for the outside world to see us as the perfect family. Every once in a while, there was tension between us that would erupt, but overall, Brad took what I dealt out. Maybe he recognized that it was what I needed to walk through in order to grow.

This behavior wasn't just a detriment to my relationship with Brad, but especially to our first child, Nicholas. Unbeknownst to me, by communicating that he had to look a certain way, ironically, I was doing all the things to him that I felt had been put upon me as a child—because I needed to prove to my parents, to the judge, to the world that gay couples can parent. When we got Donavan a few years later, I felt this pressure even more because he's African American. With Nicholas, the world could perceive one of us as the biological father and the other one as a friend. But with Donavan, we're a unit of four, and it's very clear we're a same-sex couple with adopted children. I felt like we had to try even harder to look acceptable as a family.

A turning point came during the pandemic in 2020. We spent a lot of time with each other, locked down. Schooling was very exhausting and frustrating for everyone. I'd worked from home since

2003, but now my business had to shift to a virtual model, so I was learning a new way of hosting events remotely. Nicholas, fourteen at that time, was struggling with online bullying, as well as things that had happened in his life prior to the pandemic. Now, we were all isolated and no longer had access to friends, so we were forced to face our emotions.

When I started to see Nicholas's downturn, I didn't know what to do, other than to just be there for him and help him by giving him the resources that he needed through therapy. The recommendation was that despite our fears of COVID-19, the kids should go back to school in person. It wasn't good, particularly for Nicholas, to stay at home; isolation posed a greater risk to his mental health than the virus did to his physical health. So, we let them go back to school, and it was at that moment that Nicholas wanted to have some self-expression, which looked like dyeing his hair.

I started putting all of what I went through as a child onto Nicholas, not giving him permission to be himself. I wanted to protect him. I wanted him not to go through what I'd gone through. I already knew he had experienced so much anxiety, people were calling him derogatory terms, and he was internalizing all those messages. I could see it all happening. Rather than giving him permission to be himself and supporting him, I was telling him, "No, you can't dye your hair," or "No, you can't wear those types of clothes," or "You can do that in the house, but you can't do that in the world."

I was being exactly like my mom: *You can be who you want to be in the safe house, but when you're out in the world, you have to pretend that you're something different, because the world is not going to be kind to you.* With time to reflect during lockdown, it hit me that I have to allow him to be who he is, and I have to give the same to Donavan. And that involves not only giving permission but also giving an education. Living in Florida, particularly during this turbulent time for civil rights and LGBTQIA+ rights, we need to share with our children where our fears come from and educate our youth on the progress we've witnessed over the years. As a parent, I've learned that permission is sometimes hard because you want to protect the ones you love.

After I realized I hadn't been giving our children full permission to be themselves, I started thinking about my relationship with Brad. Was I giving Brad permission to be himself? The answer was that I was not. I was repeating history, perpetuating patterns, treating others the way I was treated. Those patterns were so unconsciously internalized that I was projecting them onto others. Once I realized what I was doing, I sat down and told my oldest son, "You have permission to be who you are. Let me know how I can help." Our relationship has changed; he has less anger toward me. Nicholas was so angry with us, understandably so, just as I had been really angry with my mom for having been stifled.

Now I'm trying to apply that to all of my relationships—being open to letting people I love and adore be who they are. Slowly, this has included my relationship with my mom. I'm starting to see family members a bit more clearly and with less judgment. My relationships have become more honest; I appreciate the people in my life more. I try not to take so much personally, not to be concerned if I don't hear from someone for a while, and to let them speak up or reach out when they need to. And I try not to put any judgment on what they're saying; I can simply listen, instead of trying to "fix" them or shut them out. My relationships are less about me now.

I'm also advocating for myself and others more, instead of allowing toxic patterns or behaviors to continue. At a recent gathering, my mother cooked the entire family a delicious meal. I noticed how everyone left her to do the washing up, and the house was a wreck. She's seventy-six years old—she was tired! I stayed and washed all the dishes for her. Everyone had left it for her because she allowed them to. That is how it had always been. I don't blame my family at all; Mom insisted she would clean even after they asked. But frankly, she wanted the help; she just didn't know how to advocate for herself. The apple doesn't fall far from the tree. I don't want to be the person who says, "No, you don't have to do that." Yes, we need help.

It was in a therapy session when the word "permission" came up—that I was looking for permission to be myself. It was an *aha* moment. I needed to give others permission to be whoever they are, and then love them for who they are, rather than who

I want them to be. That's what I wanted all along as a child. What I would tell Tracy the child is to jump out and give yourself permission to be you. Demand respect. Don't allow others to stop you from achieving greatness.

The message that I would tell my seven-year-old self at Christmas is: "Get out there and say, 'I don't want this truck—I want the Easy-Bake oven!'" Society accepts confidence. I look at Ross Mathews, who rose to fame as the effeminate, gay roving reporter on *The Tonight Show*. He is not asking for anyone's permission to be himself. I think of my friend Daron, who was a male cheerleader not afraid to put himself out there, wearing the short shorts with his butt cheeks sticking out. He was adored. He gave himself permission to be who he wanted to be. That's what I did not do. I was seeking external permission. If I could do this life over again, I would tell my little self, "Just be you. You were born to be seen."

Epilogue

As an adult going through therapy, I learned that when someone feels they are unable to be who they are, if there is a space where they can be themselves even for a short amount of time, that window of opportunity can prevent suicidal ideation. For me, that space was Granny's studio.

I hope that you, dear reader, have your own "Granny's studio"—a safe space and outlet where you can let loose and be yourself in ways you may not feel able to in other environments, like school or work. I hope that, in some small way, you may have found a healthy escape within the pages of this book. Maybe you can relate to some of the situations in my story and have taken away from this story that everything is temporary—especially high school!

You have the power within yourself to ask for what you need—to demand to be seen. And whether or not your family or the outside world has given you permission to be who you are, *you don't need it*. It's great to have it—especially as a child—but at some point, you need to give yourself permission, first and foremost. You can't choose your parents, but there are a lot of other choices you can make in life: where you work, who you date, who you hang out with, how you parent your own kids. Check in with yourself—are you giving everyone else permission to be themselves? You may find that once you give *them* permission, they will give it to you, too. Remember, you are worthy—of being celebrated, of being loved, of being seen.

As this book comes to an end, I want to share a message of inclusivity, strength, resilience, and courage. Sure, there is still much work to be done in terms of eradication of hate and violence, but I believe the progress made since my upbringing in rural Ohio in the 1970s has been remarkable. For many, the freedom to be seen, exist, and express themselves has enabled a new level of self-realization and acceptance. There is an ever-growing sense of community among gender-nonconforming individuals, as more and more people are speaking openly about their gender identity. Let's not lose what we've gained; as the world is becoming more troubling, we need to stand up and give permission to ourselves and give permission to marginalized populations around the world.

Despite all the injustices experienced by gender-nonconforming individuals, there is still a dawn of optimism and hope. Those who have bravely stood up for their rights are beginning to be heard, and this momentum gives me hope that our society will continue to move toward a more tolerant and enlightened future. On that note, I want to acknowledge everyone who has contributed to making our world just a little bit brighter. Keep raising the torch, and keep going until we reach a place where all can truly be free to express themselves and be seen.

For those who are struggling, do not give up—you are not alone, and the future you create is within your reach. We all deserve a place in this world. It's not an accident that we are here, and we deserve to be seen.

Acknowledgments

I would like to express my deepest appreciation to my husband for supporting me on all my journeys since being together, including writing this book.

I would also like to extend my deepest gratitude to my mom, my dad, my stepmom, my granny and grandpa, my grandmother and grandfather, and so many others in my family who gave me those moments in my childhood to be me!

I cannot begin to express my thanks to the many individuals who have nurtured my passions, coached me, and given me the opportunities that have allowed me to live such a rich life.

Special thanks to Karen Rowe and her team for helping me write this book and share my story.

And finally to my boys—I hope you both will follow your passion and not be afraid to give yourself permission to be all that you can be!

ABOUT
the Author

Trace Kingham is an event strategist with over twenty-five years of experience producing live and streaming events and conferences across the country. Having received many national and international awards for his work, Trace has helped numerous organizations develop deeper connections with audiences through strategic environments, creative programming, and inspirational video productions. He's most passionate about helping his clients raise critical funding to provide lifesaving services to members of communities in need. He's passionate about connecting communities to his clients' organizations to improve community awareness of their services.

Trace founded Reimagined Experiences, his event strategy firm in Tampa, Florida, in June 2014, which has produced events for many widely recognized local and national organizations, including the American Red Cross, St. Pete Free Clinic, Girls Scouts, and Lutheran Social Services, just to name a few.

Trace has served as chair of the Tampa Bay LGBT Chamber, which is the premier voice of the Greater Tampa Bay LGBTQ+ business community, representing more than six hundred businesses, community groups, and individuals in seven counties. Trace has also served as a board member for the Heart Gallery of Pinellas and Pasco, an agency that helps find forever homes for children in the foster care system.

Appendix

THERAPIST NOTES

I asked Angie Speller, LMHC, an experienced licensed mental health counselor, for some input around self-permission. Her master's degree in mental health, and marriage and family counseling inform these practical solutions to find permission to be yourself.

Self-Reflection and Awareness

Take time to understand yourself and your strengths, passions, and values. Reflect on your past experiences, and identify the moments when you felt truly alive and fulfilled.

Embracing Your Authenticity

Embrace your uniqueness, and let go of the need for approval or conformity. Embracing who you truly are enables you to tap into your strengths and talents. There is power in being genuine and unapologetically yourself.

Passion and Purpose

Aligning your actions with your passions and values empowers you to make a meaningful impact on your life and the lives of others.

Overcoming Fear and Limiting Beliefs

Unleashing your power requires confronting and overcoming fear and limiting beliefs. Understand that fear is a natural part of growth, but it should never hold you back. Challenge the negative beliefs that undermine your confidence, and replace them with the mindset that anything is possible. Be your own cheerleader.

Taking Action

Power without action remains dormant. Take pro-active steps toward your goals and dreams. Each action you take strengthens your sense of personal power and propels you closer to your vision. Celebrate each step.

Surrounding Yourself with Support

Seek out a supportive network of friends, mentors, or like-minded individuals who uplift and inspire you. Surrounding yourself with positive influences fuels your power and provides encouragement along your journey.

Milton Keynes UK
Ingram Content Group UK Ltd.
UKHW031042120324
439302UK00001B/47